D1002906
THUNDER AGENTS
VOLUME ONE

VOLUME ONE

NICK **SPENCER**
writer

CAFU BIT
CHRISCROSS HOWARD **CHAYKIN**
GEORGE **PÉREZ** SCOTT **KOBLISH**
RYAN **SOOK** MIKE **GRELL** NICK **DRAGOTTA**
DAN **PANOSIAN** DAN **McDAID**
artists

SANTIAGO **ARCAS** BRAD **ANDERSON**
JESUS **ABURTOV BLOND** RYAN **SOOK**
VAL **STAPLES** LEE **LOUGHRIDGE**
colorists

SWANDS PAT **BROSSEAU**
JARED K. **FLETCHER**
letterers

FRANK **QUITELY** & VAL **STAPLES**
after Wally Wood
cover

T.H.U.N.D.E.R. AGENTS PROJECT initiated by MICHAEL **USLAN**

WIL **MOSS** Editor – Original Series
DAVID M. **MATTHEWS** Editorial Consultant – Original Series
IAN **SATTLER** Director Editorial, Special Projects and Archival Editions
ROBBIN **BROSTERMAN** Design Director – Books
ROBBIE **BIEDERMAN** Publication Design

EDDIE **BERGANZA** Executive Editor
BOB **HARRAS** VP – Editor in Chief

DIANE **NELSON** President
DAN **DIDIO** and JIM **LEE** Co-Publishers
GEOFF **JOHNS** Chief Creative Officer
JOHN **ROOD** Executive VP – Sales, Marketing and Business Development
AMY **GENKINS** Senior VP – Business and Legal Affairs
NAIRI **GARDINER** Senior VP – Finance
JEFF **BOISON** VP – Publishing Operations
MARK **CHIARELLO** VP – Art Direction and Design
JOHN **CUNNINGHAM** VP – Marketing
TERRI **CUNNINGHAM** VP – Talent Relations and Services
ALISON GILL Senior VP – Manufacturing and Operations
DAVID **HYDE** VP – Publicity
HANK **KANALZ** Senior VP – Digital
JAY **KOGAN** VP – Business and Legal Affairs, Publishing
JACK **MAHAN** VP – Business Affairs, Talent
NICK **NAPOLITANO** VP – Manufacturing Administration
SUE **POHJA** VP – Book Sales
COURTNEY **SIMMONS** Senior VP – Publicity
BOB **WAYNE** Senior VP – Sales

T.H.U.N.D.E.R. AGENTS Volume One
Published by DC Comics.

DC Comics, 1700 Broadway, New York, NY 10019
A Warner Bros. Entertainment Company
Printed by RR Donnelley, Salem, VA, USA. 10/14/11. First Printing.
ISBN: 978-1-4012-3254-2

Cover by **Frank Quitely** & **Val Staples**, after **Wally Wood**

DC
T.H.U.N.D.E.R.
AGENTS
LIGHT NING
NO MAN
MEN
DYN AMO

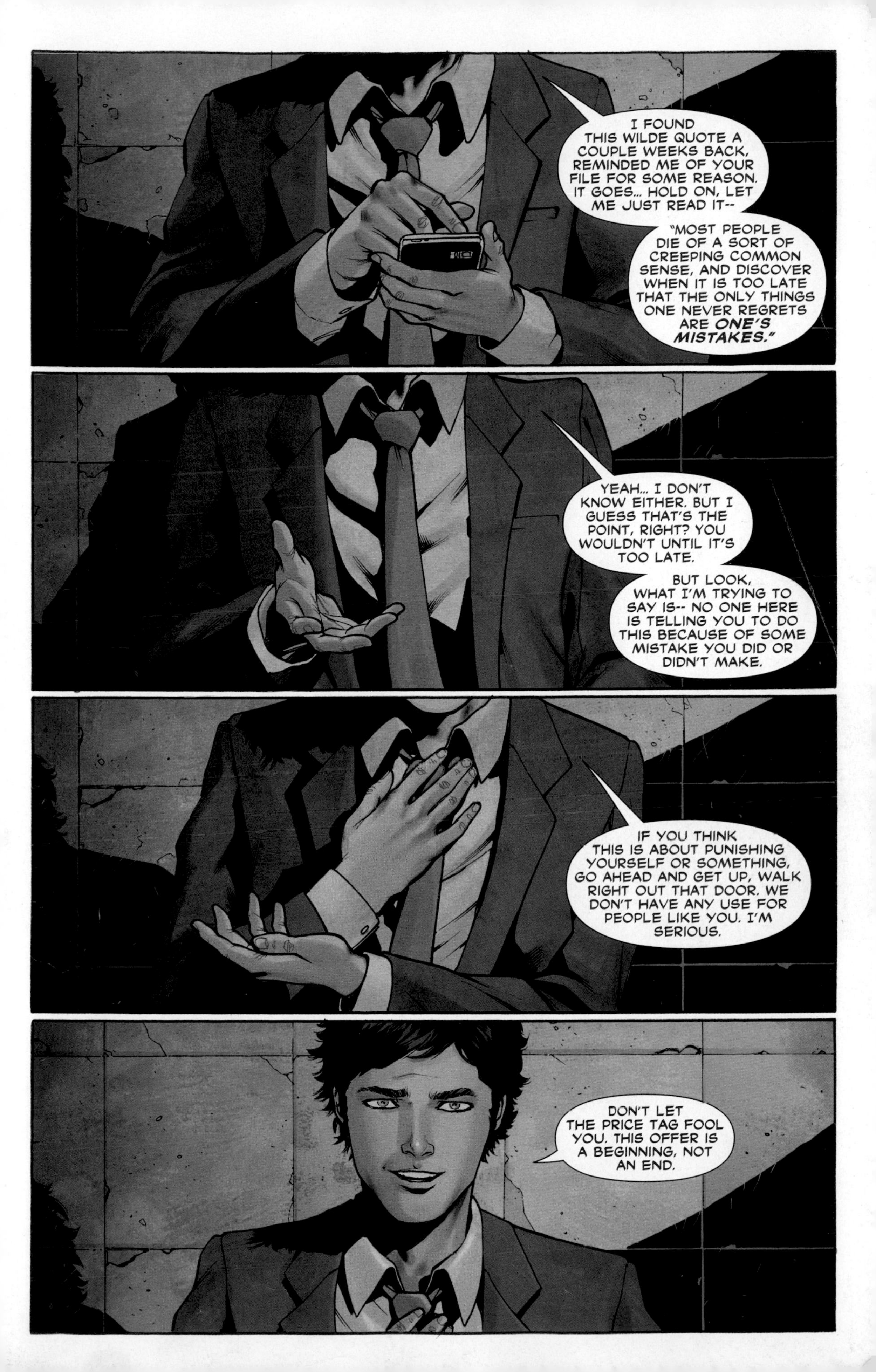
I FOUND THIS WILDE QUOTE A COUPLE WEEKS BACK, REMINDED ME OF YOUR FILE FOR SOME REASON. IT GOES... HOLD ON, LET ME JUST READ IT--
"MOST PEOPLE DIE OF A SORT OF CREEPING COMMON SENSE, AND DISCOVER WHEN IT IS TOO LATE THAT THE ONLY THINGS ONE NEVER REGRETS ARE *ONE'S MISTAKES.*"
YEAH... I DON'T KNOW EITHER. BUT I GUESS THAT'S THE POINT, RIGHT? YOU WOULDN'T UNTIL IT'S TOO LATE.
BUT LOOK, WHAT I'M TRYING TO SAY IS-- NO ONE HERE IS TELLING YOU TO DO THIS BECAUSE OF SOME MISTAKE YOU DID OR DIDN'T MAKE.
IF YOU THINK THIS IS ABOUT PUNISHING YOURSELF OR SOMETHING, GO AHEAD AND GET UP, WALK RIGHT OUT THAT DOOR. WE DON'T HAVE ANY USE FOR PEOPLE LIKE YOU. I'M SERIOUS.
DON'T LET THE PRICE TAG FOOL YOU. THIS OFFER IS A BEGINNING, NOT AN END.

HOW WAS THAT?
IT WAS **GREAT.**

DO YOU THINK WE COULD ACTUALLY LEAVE THE WOMEN'S RESTROOM AND TRY SAYING IT TO THE PROSPECT NOW?

THUNN

...IN A MINUTE.

SRI LANKA.
ELEVEN MONTHS LATER.
"DO YOU KNOW WHERE THE WORD 'SOLDIER' COMES FROM?"
IT'S FROM THE LATIN, SAL DARE. MEANS "TO GIVE SALT."
SEE, FOR A LONG TIME, SOME HISTORIANS THOUGHT THIS MEANT THAT THE ROMANS PAID THEIR SOLDIERS IN SALT. TURNS OUT THEY DIDN'T. THEY JUST GAVE THEM MONEY TO BUY RATIONS OF IT.
THAT'S ALSO WHERE THE WORD SALARY COMES FROM--SALARIUM.
BUT HERE'S THE SAD PART. THE ROMAN EMPIRE CONTROLLED THE MARKET FOR SALT--
--AND WHENEVER THEY NEEDED TO FUND A NEW WAR, THEY JUST JACKED PRICES UP FOR EVERYONE.
WHICH MEANS THOSE SOLDIERS DIED FOR LESS THE MORE THEY FOUGHT.
I'M SORRY, COLLEEN... DON'T GET ME WRONG, THAT'S VERY FASCINATING, BUT--

--PERHAPS WE SHOULD MOVE INSIDE?

AND DENY ME MY MARIE ANTOINETTE MOMENT? I DON'T THINK SO.

FINE. YOU UNDERSTAND I HAVE TO RECORD THIS?
MM.

GOOD. NOW IF IT'S ALL RIGHT, I'D LIKE TO START WITH THE ABDUCTION OF RAVEN.
I GUESS I SHOULD ASK THEN--

"--WHICH ONE?"
COLOMBIA.
TWELVE MONTHS AGO.
THERE HE IS! HURRY, HURRY!

IT IS GOOD TO SEE YOU AGAIN, BROTHER PRICE! YOUR TRIP WAS NOT TOO DIFFICULT?
I JUST TRAVELED SIXTY MILES UNDERGROUND, ASA. I HOPE YOU'RE TRYING TO BE FUNNY.

FOR THAT I'M SORRY. IT IS THE ONLY SAFE PASSAGE WE HAVE, I'M AFRAID. BUT NOW--COME, COME--
BOOM

WHAT DID THEY BRING?
BOTH OF THEIR REMAINING AGENTS, AND OVER A DOZEN SQUADRON MEMBERS.
HOW QUAINT.

IS HE IN THERE?
SEE FOR YOURSELF. BUT PLEASE, WE DO NOT HAVE MUCH TIME--

"--AND THE BATTLE IS FAR FROM OVER."
T.H.U.N.D.E.R. TOWER.
NEW YORK CITY.
THE HIGH ROAD
ALL RIGHT, PEOPLE, STATUS UPDATE.
DYNAMO IS LOOKING GOOD AT EIGHTY-FOUR OVER SEVEN. ALL VITALS ARE FINE. LIGHTNING IS FINE TOO, ALL THINGS CONSIDERED. THIRTY-NINE-SIX-FIVE. NOT BAD.
HE SHOULDN'T HAVE LOST SO MANY YEARS IN TIKRIT.
CAN'T BE HELPED NOW. MOVING ON--WHAT'S YOUR ASSESSMENT?
HONESTLY? SOMETHING'S WRONG.
I DON'T THINK THEY'RE MAKING IT TOO EASY ON US. WE *ARE* LOSING AFTER ALL.
THAT'S NOT IT. LOOK AT THE LEFT FORMATIONS ON THEIR DRONES. THEY JUST KEEP PUSHING FORWARD, THEY'RE NOT GETTING ANY-WHERE WITH IT.
THAT'S WHERE WE'VE GOT DYNAMO, NO WAY IS THAT GOING TO WORK FOR THEM.

NICK SPENCER: WRITER CAFU: PENCILLER
BIT: INKER SANTIAGO ARCAS: COLORIST SWANDS: LETTERER
THAT'S EXACTLY WHAT I'M SAYING--
SPIDER DOESN'T DO THINGS THAT DON'T WORK.
LISTEN, I UNDERSTAND YOU'RE NERVOUS. I WOULD BE TOO IF--
THAT'S NOT WHAT THIS IS.
T.H.U.N.D.E.R. -- THE HIGHER UNITED NATIONS DEFENSE ENFORCEMENT RESERVES -- IS CHARGED WITH TACKLING THE KIND OF THREATS MOST SUPERHEROES DON'T EVEN KNOW EXIST. TO ACCOMPLISH THIS, THEY EMPOWER THEIR AGENTS WITH SPECIAL ABILITIES -- ABILITIES, HOWEVER, THAT WILL EVENTUALLY KILL THEM. WHAT KIND OF MEN AND WOMEN WOULD PAY SUCH A STEEP PRICE? THESE ARE THE ...
T.H.U.N.D.E.R. AGENTS®
DID YOU TALK TO DANIEL ABOUT THIS? DON'T FORGET...

"...THE FRONTAL ATTACK IS NOT THE PRIORITY HERE."
SO THIS IS *THE RAVEN.*

PRETTY INCREDIBLE.
HE'S GOING TO BE PRETTY WORTHLESS UNLESS YOU CAN GET THE NUMBERS OUT OF HIM.

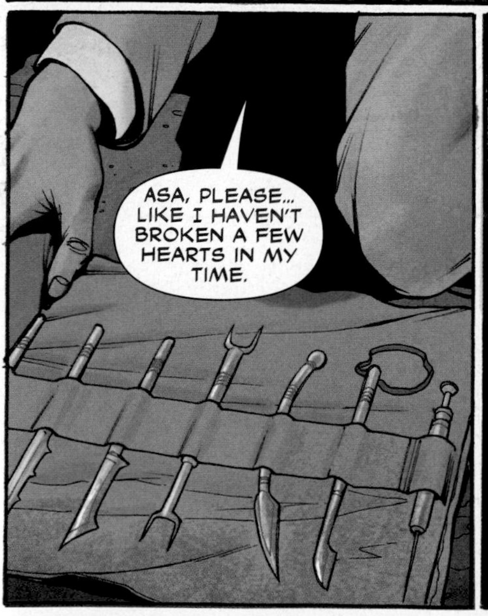
ASA, PLEASE... LIKE I HAVEN'T BROKEN A FEW HEARTS IN MY TIME.

YOU DON'T NEED TO SEDATE HIM, BROTHER. MY MEN HAVE ALREADY TAKEN CARE OF THAT.
DON'T WORRY.

IT'S NOT FOR HIM.

TOWER, THIS IS LYLE, CHECKING IN. I AM AT POINT C, ASSET IS ON-SITE--

--FACE TO FACE.
LADIES AND GENTLEMEN, WE ARE IN THE ROOM!

RAVEN! HEY, CAN YOU HEAR ME?!

GREAT.

COLLEEN! WHERE THE HELL ARE YOU GOING?

UNFFFF... COME ON, COME ON... WAKE UP...

BOOM

OKAY, OLD MAN--

TIME TO FLY.

WHY DIDN'T YOU TELL US, YOU SICK SON OF A BITCH?!?

HOW MUCH FARTHER... *HUFF*... TO THE PICKUP?

THERE.
I--I NEED TO TALK TO KEANE. THESE... UHNN... THESE SPIDER PEOPLE... THEY'RE NOT WHO WE THINK THEY ARE. THEY'RE JUST--
WAIT. WHERE IS EVERY--?

UNFFH!

SIR, OUR SIGNAL...
HOLD ON-- LYLE, WHERE'D YOU GO? WE LOST YOUR SIGNAL--

LYLE! LYLE! CAN YOU HEAR ME? YOU'RE OFF GRID, WE CAN'T--

DIRECTOR KEANE, SPIDER ONLY HAS A QUESTION: WHY DID GOD HARDEN THE PHARAOH'S HEART?

TRAP, DAMN IT. THIS IS A TRAP. GET THEM OUT OF THERE. NOW.
I'M TRYING, SIR, BUT--

"--IT'S TOO LATE."
"LIGHTNING...?"
"...HE'S GONE, SIR."
"WHAT ABOUT DYNAMO?"

ONE HUNDRED SEVENTY OVER FOUR, SIR. ACTIVATE THE KILL SWITCH?
NOT MUCH POINT IN THAT NOW, IS THERE?!?

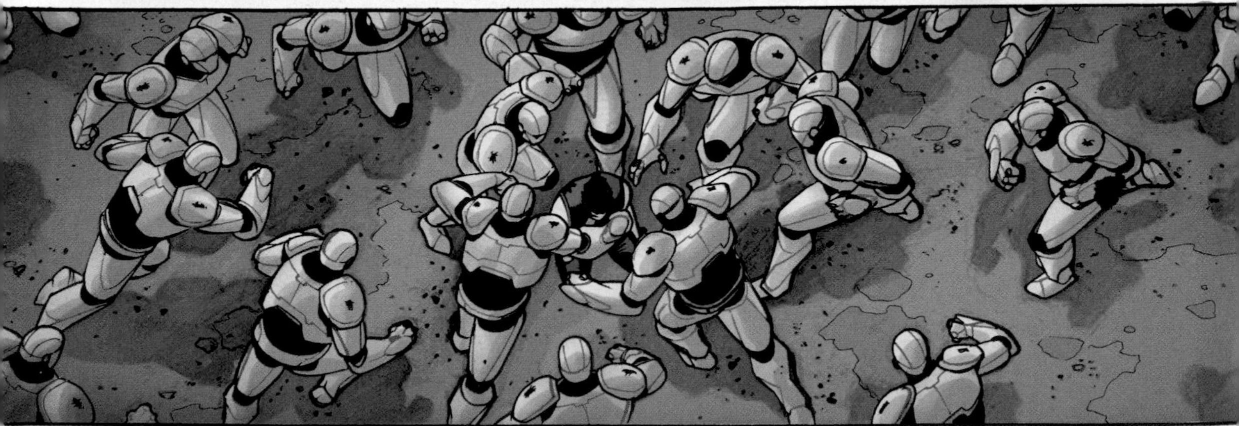

WHAT JUST HAPPENED HERE?

SOMEBODY GET ME A SALESMAN.

TOBY HENSTON.
MM.
AND YOU'D NEVER MET BEFORE THIS, CORRECT?
THAT'S RIGHT.

I UNDERSTAND YOU TWO WERE QUITE THE PAIR.

I THOUGHT HE WAS A COMPLETE IDIOT.

OKAY, LET ME SEE IF I UNDERSTAND THIS. RAVEN GOT KIDNAPPED.
YES.

BY WHO?
BY *SPIDER.*

SO THEN WE WENT IN TO RESCUE HIM, AND HE ENDED UP GETTING KIDNAPPED AGAIN... WHO DID IT THIS TIME?
SPIDER.

BUT... YOU'RE SAYING *SPIDER* KIDNAPPED HIM FROM THEMSELVES.
EXACTLY.

AND... ONE OF OUR GUYS DID IT?
ONE OF OUR GUYS WAS ONE OF THEIR GUYS.

WOW. OKAY, BUT... HOW DID THEY DO IT?

THE SQUAD COMMANDER IN QUESTION, RICHARD LYLE, TOOK OVER THE IDENTITY OF A MISSING SPIDER INTERROGATIONS OFFICER NAMED DYLAN PRICE--
--SOMEONE WITH PREVIOUS TIES TO THIS PARTICULAR SOUTH AMERICAN CELL.
LYLE, R.
PRICE, D. -SPIDER INTERROGATIONS OFFICER -WHEREAB UNKNOWN
EXCEPT?

LYLE WASN'T LYLE.
WELL, WHO WAS HE THEN?

YOU GOTTA BE KIDDING ME!

JUST... LET ME SEE IF I UNDERSTAND THIS: YOU DISGUISED THIS LYLE GUY AS PRICE, BUT PRICE WAS ACTUALLY ALREADY DISGUISED AS LYLE?!?
AND NO ONE ELSE FINDS EVEN A LITTLE BIT OF HUMOR IN THIS? THAT'S LIKE A *GET SMART* EPISODE!

SORRY. SORRY. OKAY, BUT I STILL DON'T GET IT. I MEAN, WHEN YOU SAY HE KIDNAPPED HIM FROM THEM... I MEAN, WHY? WOULDN'T THEY JUST LET THEM WALK OUT THE DOOR?

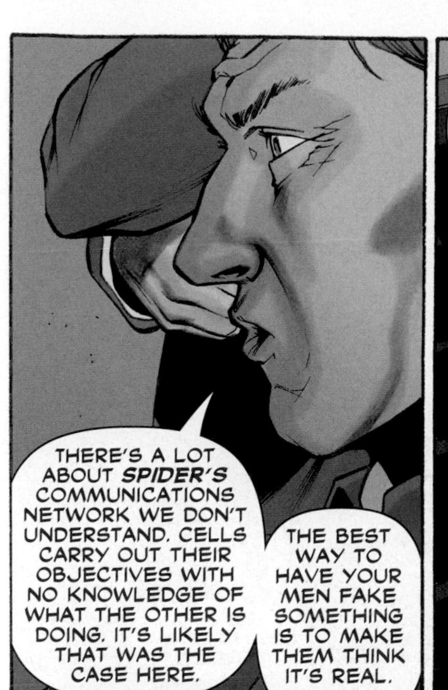
THERE'S A LOT ABOUT SPIDER'S COMMUNICATIONS NETWORK WE DON'T UNDERSTAND. CELLS CARRY OUT THEIR OBJECTIVES WITH NO KNOWLEDGE OF WHAT THE OTHER IS DOING. IT'S LIKELY THAT WAS THE CASE HERE.
THE BEST WAY TO HAVE YOUR MEN FAKE SOMETHING IS TO MAKE THEM THINK IT'S REAL.

FINE. BUT WHY KIDNAP HIM FROM THEMSELVES IN THE FIRST PLACE?
WHEN A T.H.U.N.D.E.R. ASSET GETS SNATCHED UP AND AN EXTRACTION UNIT IS DEPLOYED, CERTAIN... FAIL-SAFES ARE ACTIVATED--TRACKING CHIPS, REMOTE VIEWING LINKS, BIOMETRIC I.D. BODYSCANS--

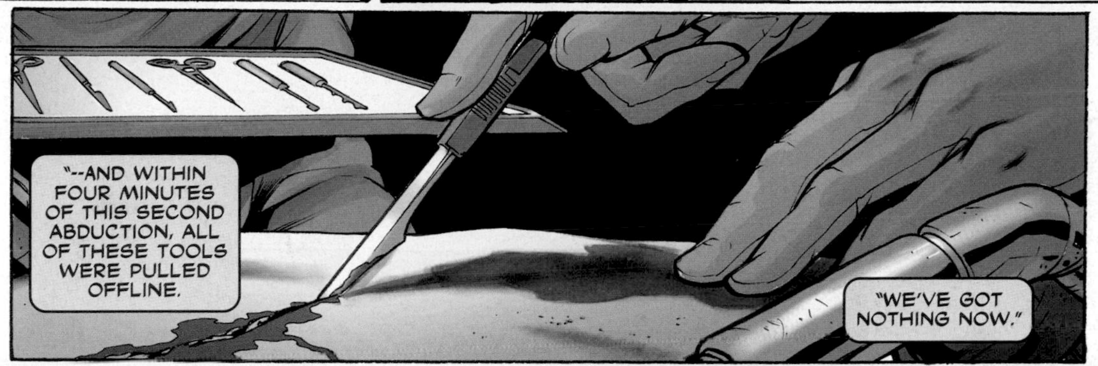
"--AND WITHIN FOUR MINUTES OF THIS SECOND ABDUCTION, ALL OF THESE TOOLS WERE PULLED OFFLINE.
"WE'VE GOT NOTHING NOW."

SO YOU'RE SAYING THEY ONLY KIDNAPPED HIM THE FIRST TIME SO THAT THEY COULD SEE WHAT YOU WOULD DO TO GET HIM BACK, THEN THEY TOOK HIM AGAIN, THIS TIME USING YOUR OWN STUFF?
AND NOW YOU HAVE NO WAY TO GET HIM BACK?
JESUS. EITHER THESE GUYS ARE GREAT, OR WE JUST REALLY, REALLY SUCK.
CAN'T IT BE BOTH?

WHERE'S THOMASON?
AH, GOOD. TOBY, I WANT YOU TO MEET COLLEEN FRANKLIN. COLLEEN IS THE FIELD AGENT YOU'LL BE WORKING WITH ON THIS.
THIS IS THE SALESMAN? DOES HE EVEN KNOW WHAT *THIS* IS?
UH-OH. NEW PARTNER TENSION.

WE'RE PUTTING TOGETHER ANOTHER EXTRACTION UNIT. SIMPLY PUT, RAVEN HAS SPECIFIC... *INFORMATION* WE'RE NOT WILLING TO LET GO OF JUST YET.

GREAT. WELL, LOAD UP DYNAMO AND LIGHTNING, I CAN GET US SOME NEW SQUADRON SIGNUPS IF THAT'S WHAT YOU--
DYNAMO AND LIGHTNING ARE DEAD.

WHAT?
THEY DIDN'T COME BACK FROM COLOMBIA.

YOU'RE HERE, TOBY, BECAUSE WE NEED NEW T.H.U.N.D.E.R. AGENTS.
SERIOUSLY? ME?

THE AGENT INITIATIVE HAS BEEN THE CROWN JEWEL OF THE HIGHER UNITED NATIONS EFFORT SINCE BEFORE EITHER OF YOU WERE BORN.
WE HANDLE GLOBAL-LEVEL THREATS HERE, THREATS THAT GO ABOVE SECURITY COUNCIL CLEARANCES, AND THE AGENTS ARE OUR FIRST RESPONSE. WE NEED THE BEST OF THE BEST.

UNFORTUNATELY, THE EQUIPMENT THAT EMPOWERS THE AGENTS CAN ONLY BE USED EFFECTIVELY BY A HANDFUL OF PEOPLE.
DIVIDE THAT BY THE NUMBER OF PEOPLE WILLING AND QUALIFIED FOR THIS KIND OF WORK, AND IDENTIFYING SUITABLE CANDIDATES BECOMES A SERIOUS CHALLENGE.
SO... HOW DO YOU FIND THEM, THEN?

D
WE DON'T.

WE ASK DANIEL.

SINCE THE 1970s, VARIOUS GOVERNMENTAL INTELLIGENCE AGENCIES HAVE USED ALGORITHMS TO DETERMINE THE SELECTION OF NEW AGENTS FOR COVERT WORK.
DANIEL TAKES THAT BILLIONS OF STEPS FURTHER. QUANTUM COMPUTING, ARTIFICIAL INTELLIGENCE, AND UNLIMITED ACCESS TO ALL THE WORLD'S STORED INFORMATION COME TOGETHER TO CREATE "THE GOD MACHINE."
HE REPRESENTS FREEDOM FROM UNCERTAINTY AND HUMAN ERROR. YOU CAN ASK HIM ANYTHING. WEATHER PATTERNS, GLOBAL PANDEMICS, TERRORIST ATTACKS--
--DANIEL CAN ANSWER ANY QUESTION YOU HAVE.
AND YOU ALREADY ASKED WHO WE SHOULD--
IDNANI, S.
MENTHOR
LINDAHL, E.
DYNAMO
COSGEI, H.
LIGHTNING
THESE ARE OUR MEN.
HM. GONNA NEED ONE HELL OF A PITCH FOR THIS ONE.

WHAT'S A PITCH?
LET ME ASK YOU SOMETHING--LET'S SAY YOU FOUND YOURSELF STUCK IN A VERY BAD PLACE. I DON'T MEAN YOU'RE HAVING A BAD DAY, OR YOU HATE YOUR JOB, OR SOMETHING STUPID LIKE THAT.
"I MEAN SOMETHING YOU CAN'T DIG YOUR WAY OUT OF. SOME MISTAKE, SOME REGRET THAT HAUNTS YOU, EVERY SECOND OF EVERY DAY OF YOUR LIFE.
"YOU KEEP TRYING TO FIND SOME WAY TO ESCAPE IT. YOU KEEP TRYING TO RUN AWAY FROM IT.
"BUT INSTEAD IT JUST BECOMES YOUR PRISON. AND ALL YOU'RE LEFT TO DO IS SIT THERE, DROWNING IN YOUR OWN GUILT AND SHAME, WAITING TO DIE--*WANTING* TO DIE.

"THEN LET'S SAY, JUST WHEN YOU WERE AT YOUR LOWEST POINT, SOMEONE CAME TO YOU AND OFFERED YOU A CHOICE.
"A CHANCE TO CHANGE EVERYTHING. A WAY TO REDEEM YOURSELF, TO REWRITE YOUR OWN HISTORY...TO MAKE THE WORLD--TO MAKE YOURSELF--FORGET YOUR PAST.
"BUT EVEN MORE THAN THAT, A CHANCE TO DO GREAT THINGS, THINGS MOST PEOPLE CAN ONLY DREAM OF.
"A CHANCE TO BE A HERO. TO SAVE THE WORLD."
AND THIS IS WHAT WE DID. WE GAVE THEM THAT CHOICE. AND ONCE THEY ACCEPTED OUR OFFER--

"WE EQUIPPED THEM...
"WE TRAINED THEM...

"WE SENT THEM IN TO RESCUE **RAVEN** AND DESTROY **SPIDER...**"

AND THEN WE KILLED THEM.
ALL OF THEM.

Cover by Gary Frank & Brad Anderson, after Wally Wood

SRI LANKA.
NOW.
SO WHEN WE DROP DOWN THERE, BIG QUESTION IS GONNA BE HOW LONG WILL IT TAKE HIM TO HIT THE PACES--AND IF IT'S OVER FIVE, WE'LL HAVE TO ADJUST TO THAT AND--HEY--
--YOU NEED TO PAY ATTENTION TO THIS, TOBY.
NO, HEY, I AM, I AM-- IT'S JUST--

--I GOTTA FIND "FORTUNATE SON" ON MY iPOD BEFORE WE'RE NOT IN THIS HELICOPTER ANYMORE...

MANY PEOPLE KNOW THAT KENYANS ARE, WITHOUT QUESTION, THE BEST RUNNERS IN THE WORLD. BUT WHAT MANY DO NOT KNOW IS THAT MOST OF THOSE GREAT RUNNERS ACTUALLY HAIL FROM A TINY TRIBE OF FARMERS WITHIN THE COUNTRY CALLED THE KALENJIN.
"MR. FOGG HAD NOT TIME TO STOP THE BRAVE FELLOW, WHO, OPENING A DOOR UNPERCEIVED BY THE INDIANS, SUCCEEDED IN SLIPPING UNDER THE CAR--"
AROUND THE WORLD IN EIGHTY DAYS
ACCOUNTING FOR LESS THAN 0.001 PERCENT OF THE WORLD POPULATION, THEY HAVE WON OVER SEVENTY PERCENT OF ALL MAJOR PRIZES IN LONG DISTANCE RUNNING SINCE THE 1930s.
SINCE 1964, KALENJIN RUNNERS ALONE ARE RESPONSIBLE FOR TWENTY-SIX OLYMPIC MEDAL WINS IN TRACK, MORE THAN THE NEXT THREE COUNTRIES COMBINED.
IT IS AN ACHIEVEMENT UNRIVALED, UNMATCHED, EVEN UNIMAGINED ANYWHERE ELSE IN SPORT.

NOW, IF YOU ASK A GENETICIST WHY THEY ARE SUCH SUPERIOR RUNNERS, THEY WILL TALK OF LEAN BODY FRAMES AND SLENDER LOWER LEGS, OR THE EFFECT OF NATURAL SELECTION IN A CATTLE-HERDING CULTURE.
"--AND WHILE THE STRUGGLE CONTINUED, AND THE BALLS WHIZZED ACROSS EACH OTHER OVER HIS HEAD, HE MADE USE OF HIS OLD ACROBATIC EXPERIENCE--"

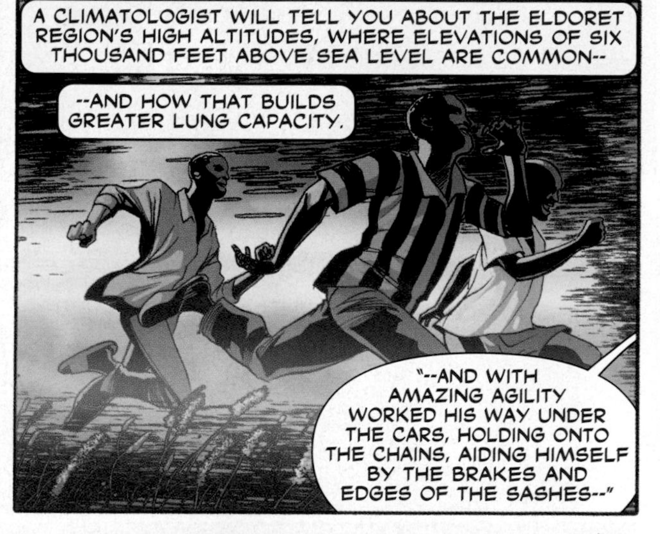
A CLIMATOLOGIST WILL TELL YOU ABOUT THE ELDORET REGION'S HIGH ALTITUDES, WHERE ELEVATIONS OF SIX THOUSAND FEET ABOVE SEA LEVEL ARE COMMON--
--AND HOW THAT BUILDS GREATER LUNG CAPACITY.
"--AND WITH AMAZING AGILITY WORKED HIS WAY UNDER THE CARS, HOLDING ONTO THE CHAINS, AIDING HIMSELF BY THE BRAKES AND EDGES OF THE SASHES--"

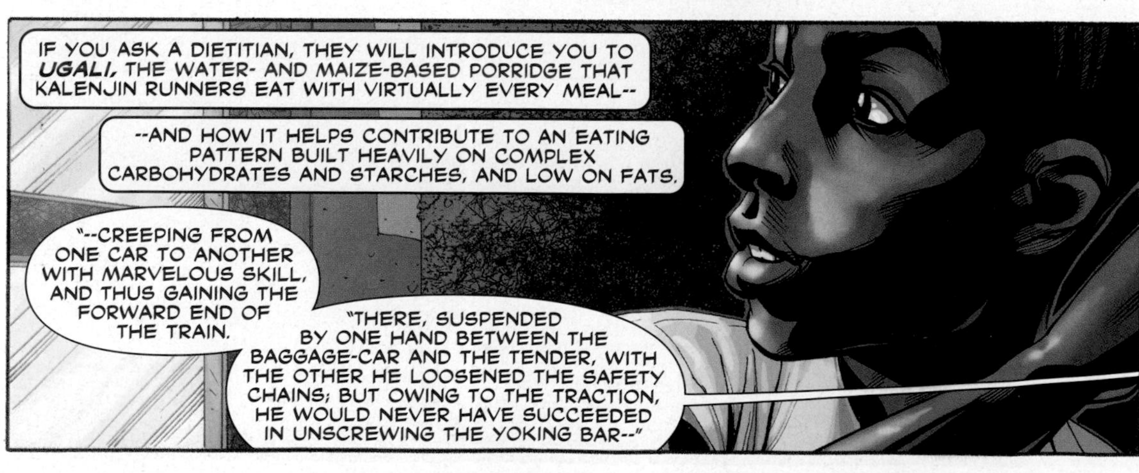
IF YOU ASK A DIETITIAN, THEY WILL INTRODUCE YOU TO UGALI, THE WATER- AND MAIZE-BASED PORRIDGE THAT KALENJIN RUNNERS EAT WITH VIRTUALLY EVERY MEAL--
--AND HOW IT HELPS CONTRIBUTE TO AN EATING PATTERN BUILT HEAVILY ON COMPLEX CARBOHYDRATES AND STARCHES, AND LOW ON FATS.
"--CREEPING FROM ONE CAR TO ANOTHER WITH MARVELOUS SKILL, AND THUS GAINING THE FORWARD END OF THE TRAIN.
"THERE, SUSPENDED BY ONE HAND BETWEEN THE BAGGAGE-CAR AND THE TENDER, WITH THE OTHER HE LOOSENED THE SAFETY CHAINS; BUT OWING TO THE TRACTION, HE WOULD NEVER HAVE SUCCEEDED IN UNSCREWING THE YOKING BAR--"

AND IF YOU ASK ONE OF THE MANY AGENTS WHO MAKE A LIVING OFF THEIR WINNINGS AND ENDORSEMENT DEALS--
--THEY MIGHT WALK YOU AROUND THE AREA AND LET YOU SEE THE POVERTY THAT CONSUMES IT, SO THAT YOU UNDERSTAND HOW THE LURE OF PRIZE MONEY, SCHOLARSHIPS, AND FAME CAUSES YOUNG PEOPLE TO TRAIN TIRELESSLY AND WITH THE SEVEREST OF DISCIPLINE.
BUT...
"--HAD NOT A VIOLENT CONCUSSION JOLTED THIS BAR OUT. THE TRAIN, NOW DETACHED FROM THE ENGINE, REMAINED A LITTLE BEHIND, WHILST THE LOCOMOTIVE RUSHED FORWARD WITH INCREASED SPEED."

HENRY!
IF YOU ASK THE KALENJIN THEMSELVES WHERE THIS TALENT COMES FROM--IF YOU ASK THEM WHAT ENABLES THEM TO BREAK RECORDS ONCE THOUGHT UNTOUCHABLE AND PUSH THEMSELVES TOWARDS NEWER AND GREATER HEIGHTS--
--THEY WILL TELL YOU THE TRUTH.
THE KALENJIN RUNS SO WELL...
...BECAUSE HE LOVES TO.
LIVE FAST, DIE YOUNG
NICK SPENCER: WRITER
CAFU: PENCILLER
BIT: INKER
SANTIAGO ARCAS: COLORIST
[Main Sequence]
CHRISCROSS: ARTIST
BRAD ANDERSON: COLORIST
[Lightning Sequence]
SWANDS: LETTERER

T.H.U.N.D.E.R. TOWER.
THEN.
HE'S A JACKASS.
COLLEEN, HE'S THE BEST WE'VE GOT.
WHAT HAPPENED TO THOMASON?
WHAT DO YOU THINK? HE WENT PRIVATE. IT'S A THIN BENCH THESE DAYS, YOU KNOW THAT.
THIS GUY'S TOO YOUNG.
...HE'S A YEAR YOUNGER THAN YOU.
I'M NOT THE ONE WHO HAS TO TALK TO THEM.
DID YOU READ THE FILE? DID YOU SEE WHAT HE DID FOR THE U.S. GUYS IN BOLIVIA?
OH, I READ IT. QUELLING ANTI-WESTERN SENTIMENT USING VIRAL-BASED LITERACY PROGRAMS--GOOD STUFF. HAS NOTHING TO DO WITH THE FACE-TO-FACE.
I WANT YOU TO BE HONEST WITH ME HERE--IF I TOLD YOU DANIEL DIDN'T PICK HIM, WOULDN'T YOU SUDDENLY BE FINE WITH WORKING WITH HIM THEN?

OKAY, TOBY, YOU READY TO GET STARTED?
I AM *EXCITED.*

WE'LL START WITH LIGHTNING, THEN.
HOW DOES THE SUIT WORK?
EXCUSE ME?

HOW DOES LIGHTNING'S SUIT WORK?
THAT'S NOT SOMETHING YOU NEED TO--
IF I'M GONNA SELL SOMETHING, I NEED TO KNOW WHAT IT IS FIRST.

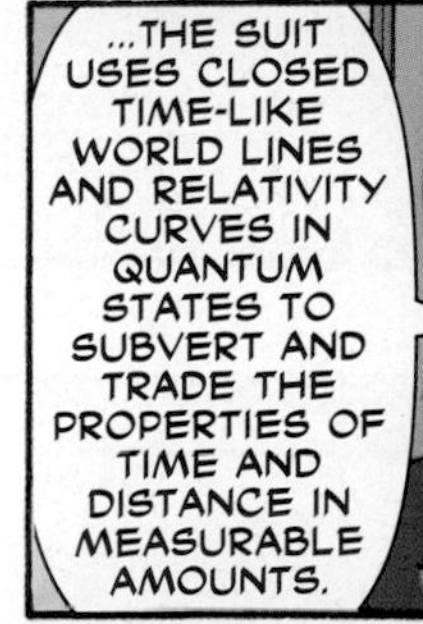
...THE SUIT USES CLOSED TIME-LIKE WORLD LINES AND RELATIVITY CURVES IN QUANTUM STATES TO SUBVERT AND TRADE THE PROPERTIES OF TIME AND DISTANCE IN MEASURABLE AMOUNTS.

YEAH, THAT'S EXACTLY HOW I'LL EXPLAIN IT TO THE PROSPECT--HE'LL GO FOR THAT, RIGHT?

THE SUIT LETS YOU RUN REAL FAST, BUT WHEN YOU USE IT, IT SHORTENS YOUR LIFE.
WAIT, I *KNOW* THIS GUY!

HENRY COSGEI HAS WON TWO OLYMPIC GOLD MEDALS AND THREE WORLD CHAMPIONSHIPS. HE HOLDS THE RECORD TIME IN THE BOSTON MARATHON.
HE IS THE GREATEST RUNNER OF HIS GENERATION.

HE LOVES EARNING THE ACCEPTANCE AND RESPECT OF HIS PEERS.

HE LOVES THE WEALTH AND THE FAME EACH WIN PROVIDES.
Wood & Brown Savings
Henry Cosgei
DOLLARS

HE LOVES THAT SPARKLE IN HIS WIFE'S EYES, THE WAY HER HAND FITS IN HIS.
HE LOVES HOLDING HIS CHILDREN CLOSE IN THE NIGHT.
HE LOVES THE SMILES ON THEIR FACES WHEN HE COMES HOME.
BUT MORE THAN ANYTHING ELSE...
HENRY COSGEI LOVES TO *RUN.*

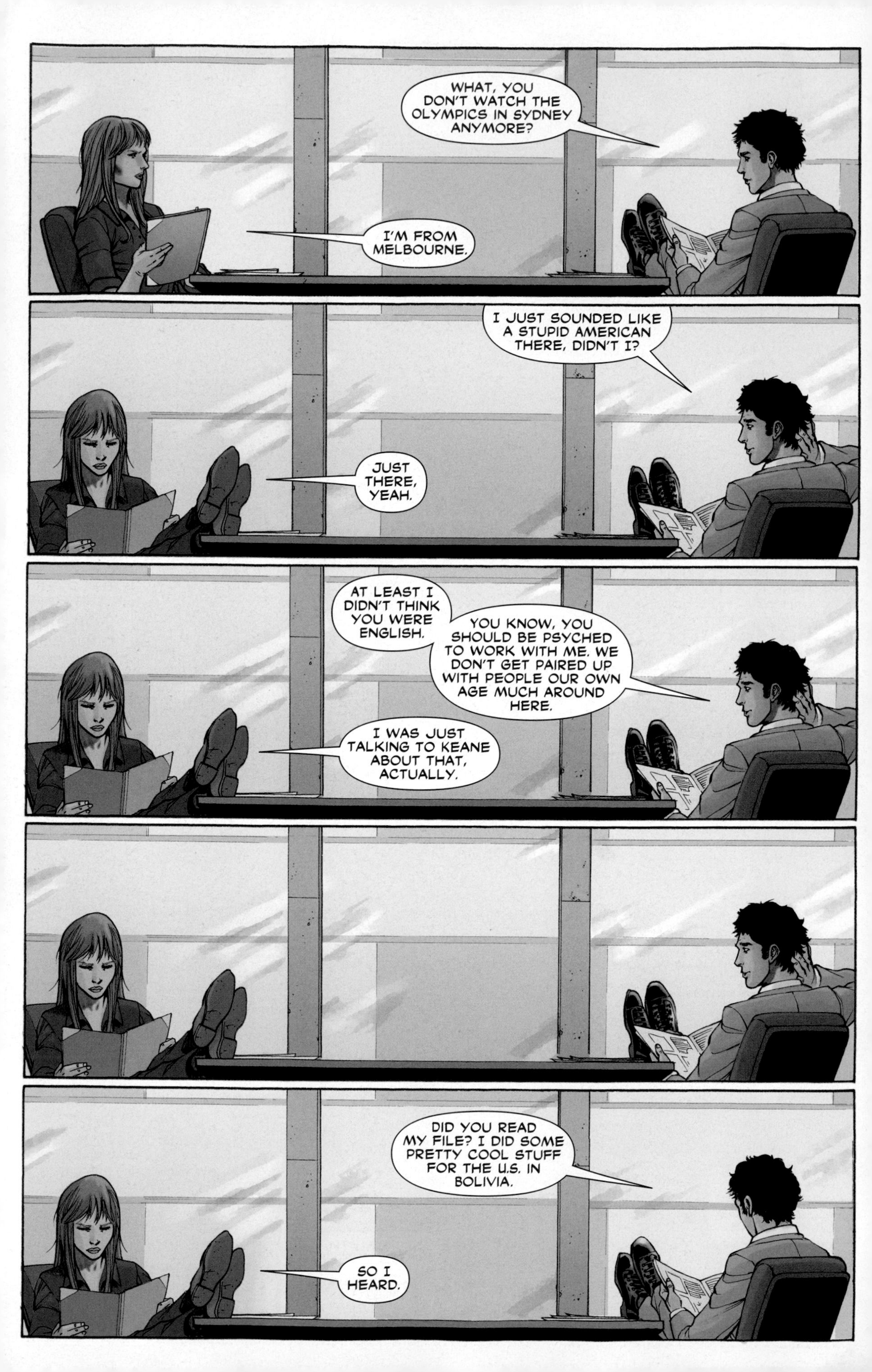
WHAT, YOU DON'T WATCH THE OLYMPICS IN SYDNEY ANYMORE?
I'M FROM MELBOURNE.
I JUST SOUNDED LIKE A STUPID AMERICAN THERE, DIDN'T I?
JUST THERE, YEAH.
AT LEAST I DIDN'T THINK YOU WERE ENGLISH.
YOU KNOW, YOU SHOULD BE PSYCHED TO WORK WITH ME. WE DON'T GET PAIRED UP WITH PEOPLE OUR OWN AGE MUCH AROUND HERE.
I WAS JUST TALKING TO KEANE ABOUT THAT, ACTUALLY.
DID YOU READ MY FILE? I DID SOME PRETTY COOL STUFF FOR THE U.S. IN BOLIVIA.
SO I HEARD.

HOW DO YOU WANT TO COME AT THIS GUY?
HMM...
THE AGENT IS THE MOST STRAIGHTFORWARD ROUTE. FAMILY WOULD BE PRETTY EASY, TOO...
DO YOU EVER FEEL GUILTY ABOUT THIS? I MEAN, WE'RE BASICALLY *KILLING* THESE GUYS.
THE INITIATIVE IS ENTIRELY VOLUNTEER. IT'S THEIR CHOICE.
THAT'S A JOKE, RIGHT?
PRETTY MUCH, YEAH.

MR. COSGEI?
YOU CAN COME RIGHT IN.

DO YOU UNDERSTAND WHY YOU'RE HERE, MR. COSGEI?
THERE WAS SOME CONFUSION-- ABOUT MY LAST TEST--
WELL, I WOULDN'T CALL IT CONFUSION. YOU TESTED POSITIVE FOR THREE BANNED SUBSTANCES IN TWO SEPARATE TESTS, SIR--
NO--
SIR, I UNDERSTAND HOW YOU MUST FEEL RIGHT NOW. AND AS LEGAL COUNSEL TO YOUR CHIEF SPONSOR, I CAN TELL YOU THAT YOU DO HAVE OPTIONS HERE.

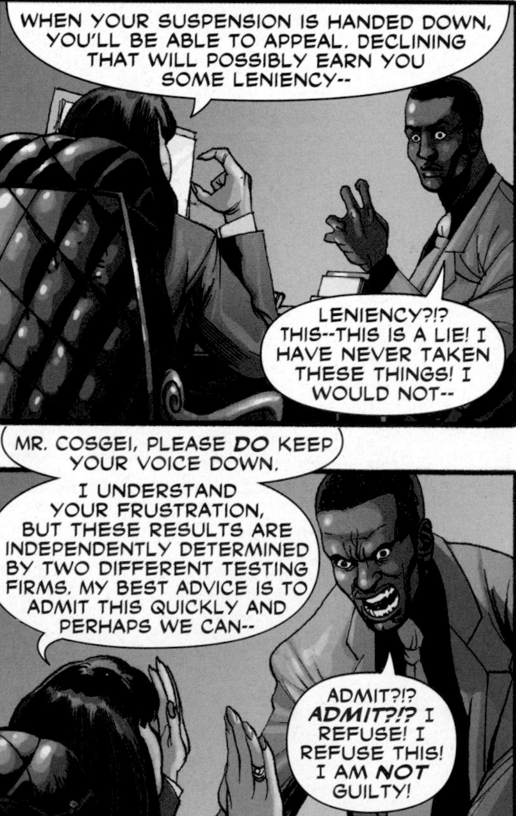
WHEN YOUR SUSPENSION IS HANDED DOWN, YOU'LL BE ABLE TO APPEAL. DECLINING THAT WILL POSSIBLY EARN YOU SOME LENIENCY--
LENIENCY?!? THIS--THIS IS A LIE! I HAVE NEVER TAKEN THESE THINGS! I WOULD NOT--
MR. COSGEI, PLEASE **DO** KEEP YOUR VOICE DOWN.
I UNDERSTAND YOUR FRUSTRATION, BUT THESE RESULTS ARE INDEPENDENTLY DETERMINED BY TWO DIFFERENT TESTING FIRMS. MY BEST ADVICE IS TO ADMIT THIS QUICKLY AND PERHAPS WE CAN--
ADMIT?!? ***ADMIT?!?*** I REFUSE! I REFUSE THIS! I AM **NOT** GUILTY!

MR. COSGEI!

10

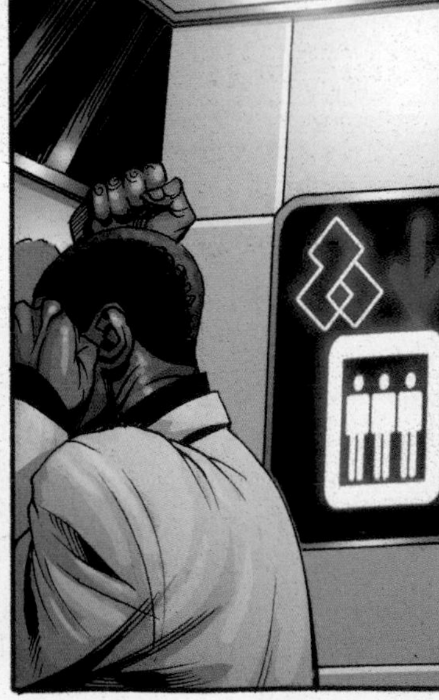
8

5

DEPARTURES
BAGGAGE CLAIM

HENRY COSGEI HAS LOST ALL THAT HE LOVED.
HE HAS BEEN STRIPPED OF HIS MEDALS.
HE FACES A THREE-YEAR SUSPENSION--LONG ENOUGH TO END HIS CAREER IN A SPORT WHERE HIS HOME COUNTRY CONSISTENTLY PRODUCES YOUNGER, FASTER RUNNERS.
HIS FORMER TEAMMATES NO LONGER SPEAK TO HIM.
HE IS BEING SUED FOR MILLIONS IN RETRACTED PRIZE MONEY. THE HOME HE BUILT FOR HIS FAMILY NOW FACES FORECLOSURE.

HE CAN NO LONGER LOOK HIS WIFE IN THE EYE.
HE GROWS DISTANT FROM HIS CHILDREN.
THERE IS A MAN HERE TO SEE YOU, HENRY.
I DO NOT WANT TO SEE ANY MORE OF THESE LAWYERS. I WILL MAKE NO APOLOGY.
I DO NOT THINK THIS ONE IS LIKE THE OTHERS.
THIS ONE SAYS YOU CAN RUN AGAIN.

OKAY, BEST INTEL HAS SPIDER ARRIVING AT THIS SITE, PRESUMABLY WITH RAVEN, TWELVE HOURS AGO--WHICH MEANS HE'S MOST LIKELY *STILL HERE.*
THEIR COMPOUND AND THE PERIMETER AROUND IT ARE EQUIPPED WITH MOTION DETECTION SENSORS THAT PICK UP ANY OBJECT THAT HITS LINE-OF-SIGHT IN .04 SECONDS.
THEY THINK THAT'S FAST ENOUGH.

IT ISN'T.

FIRST TARGET IS A GENERATOR BASE FOUR KILOMETERS AWAY FROM THE COMPOUND THAT POWERS THEIR PERIMETER DEFENSES.
WE'RE NOT THERE TO SHUT IT DOWN, JUST PINCH IT--MAKE ***THEIR*** POWER ***OUR*** POWER.
ONCE WE DO THAT, WE'LL HAVE A NARROW WINDOW OF TIME TO PLANT OUR FOOT IN THE DOOR, SO I WANT EVERYONE READY TO MOVE AT SIGNAL.
THIS IS USUALLY THE PART WHERE SOMEONE TELLS YOU HOW DANGEROUS ALL THIS IS, AND HOW SOME OF YOU WON'T MAKE IT BACK.
I PREFER TO NOT INSULT YOUR INTELLIGENCE. LET'S DO OUR JOBS.
ALL RIGHT THEN. LIGHTNING--YOU'RE UP.

YOU KNOW, I WAS GOOD FRIENDS WITH THE LAST GUY WHO WORE THIS SUIT.
I SHOULD SAY I AM VERY SORRY FOR YOUR LOSS THEN.

OKAY, LISTEN TO ME--THE SPEEDS THEY PUT YOU THROUGH IN THE TRIALS, THEY'RE NOT LIKE THIS. THEY TELL YOU IT'S THE SAME, BUT IT'S NOT.

YOU'RE GOING TO SEE THINGS. THINGS YOU DON'T **WANT** TO SEE.

AND IT'LL STOP YOU AT FIRST--
I--
--NO, TRUST ME, **IT WILL.** AND WHEN IT DOES, YOU'RE GOING TO NEED TO FORCE IT. YOU'RE GOING TO HAVE TO FOCUS.

JUST PUT ONE FOOT IN FRONT OF THE OTHER, AS FAST AS YOU CAN. JUST RUN. CAN YOU REMEMBER TO DO THAT?
MISS--

--IT IS THE ONLY THING I CAN DO.

HENRY COSGEI RUNS.
HE RUNS FASTER THAN HE EVER HAS BEFORE.
HE FEELS BETTER THAN HE HAS IN MONTHS. HE FEELS ALIVE AGAIN. FREE. HE WANTS TO ENJOY THIS, HE WANTS TO DO THIS FOREVER.

BUT THEN HE SEES WHAT THE WOMAN WARNED HIM ABOUT.
THEN HE SEES WHAT HE NEVER WANTED TO SEE.

HE IS
SEVENTY-FOUR
YEARS OLD.

HE LIES IN A BED, A
FAST-MOVING CANCER
RUSHING HIM TOWARDS
HIS LAST MOMENTS.

HIS DAUGHTER--WHO HAS BARELY
KNOWN HIM AND WITH WHOM HE
HADN'T SPOKEN IN DECADES--IS
THERE, THANKS TO A LETTER HE
SENT HER JUST A FEW WEEKS
BEFORE, IN A DESPERATE
ATTEMPT TO RECONCILE.
SHE HAS BROUGHT WITH HER HIS
GRANDCHILDREN--AND ONE GREAT
GRANDCHILD--FAMILY HE'D NEVER
KNOWN, BUT LOVED ALL THE SAME.

HE DIES
PEACEFULLY
WITH THEM
AT HIS SIDE.
HE KEEPS
RUNNING.

HE IS SEVENTY-ONE NOW. NO LETTER TO HIS DAUGHTER HAS BEEN SENT YET, AND THAT GREAT GRANDCHILD HAS YET TO BE BORN.

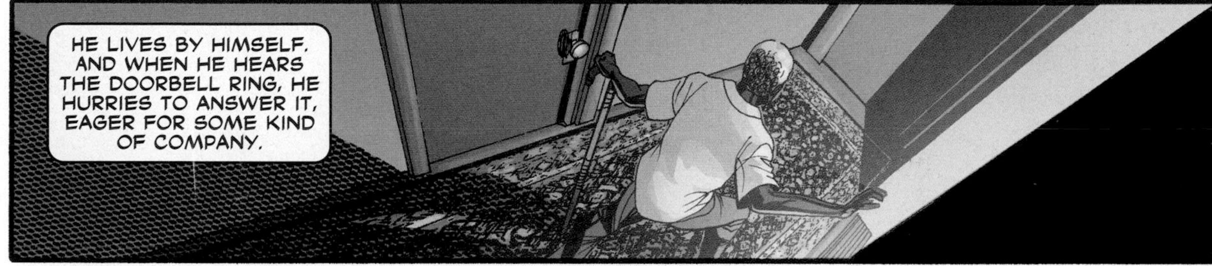
HE LIVES BY HIMSELF. AND WHEN HE HEARS THE DOORBELL RING, HE HURRIES TO ANSWER IT, EAGER FOR SOME KIND OF COMPANY.

HE USED TO BE SO FAST. IT USED TO COME SO EASILY.

HE DIES ALONE AT THE BOTTOM OF HIS STAIRS.

HE TRIES TO REMEMBER WHAT THE WOMAN TOLD HIM.
"PUT ONE FOOT IN FRONT OF THE OTHER.
"AS FAST AS YOU CAN."
HE KNOWS THAT IF HE DOES SLOW, HE WILL BE KILLED, ALONG WITH EVERYONE WHO CAME WITH HIM.

BUT HE DOESN'T WANT TO SEE THIS.

HE IS SIXTY-NINE.

THE COMPLICATIONS FROM HIS LAST SURGERY ARE SEVERE.

A NURSE SITS WITH HIM, READING TO HIM.

SHE HOLDS HIS HAND AS HE DRIFTS AWAY.

HE KEEPS RUNNING.

A WEEK EARLIER, AND HIS OPERATION HAS TAKEN A TURN FOR THE WORSE.

A TEAM OF DOCTORS WORKS FRANTICALLY TO UNDO THE DAMAGE.

BUT NOTHING CAN BE DONE.

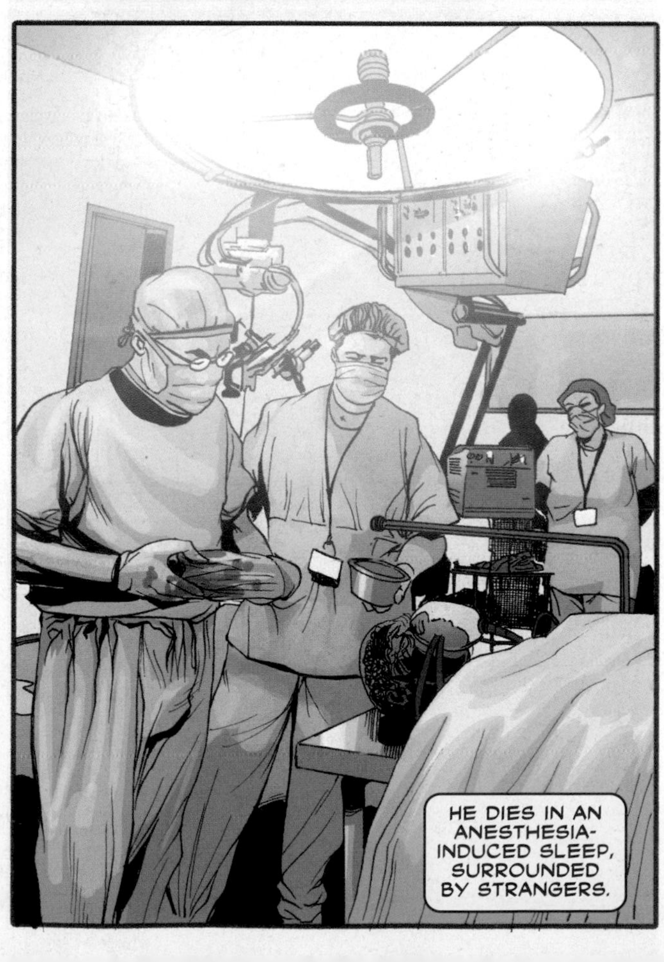
HE DIES IN AN ANESTHESIA-INDUCED SLEEP, SURROUNDED BY STRANGERS.

WITH EVERY STEP HE TAKES, HE SEES ANOTHER DEATH, EACH COMING CLOSER THAN THE LAST.
THEY TOLD HIM THAT HE COULD RUN AGAIN. THAT HE COULD BE A HERO. THAT HE COULD DO SOMETHING THAT WOULD MAKE HIS CHILDREN PROUD.
THEY TOLD HIM THAT IT WOULD HURT HIM. THAT EVERY TIME HE RAN, IT MEANT TAKING YEARS FROM HIS LIFE.
BUT THEY NEVER TOLD HIM IT WOULD BE LIKE THIS.
HENRY COSGEI STOPS RUNNING.

WE'RE IN. TWELVE MINUTES, START THE CLOCK.

WE'RE OFF TO A GOOD START HERE, THEN.
HA, YEAH. FOR A TRAP.

YOU KNOW, I WAS THINKING THE SAME THING. "BEST INTEL"--THESE GUYS ARE CUTE.

SO SINCE WE'RE WALKING RIGHT INTO IT--
--YOU WANNA TELL ME WHY YOU'RE SO CONCERN-LACKING?

"BECAUSE THIS TIME WE'VE GOT SOMETHING THEY'RE NOT EXPECTING
"THIS TIME THEY'LL NEVER SEE IT COMING."

Cover by **Chris Sprouse**, **Karl Story** & **Guy Major**,
after **Wally Wood** and **Dan Adkins**

LONDON.
THEN.
IS HE REALLY BLUE?
YES. HE IS REALLY BLUE.
AND TALL. I HEARD HE'S PRETTY TALL.
THIS IS AMAZING, RIGHT? I MEAN, WE'RE MEETING NOMAN. ONE OF THE ORIGINALS. THE REAL DEAL.
I KNOW EXACTLY WHAT I'M GONNA SAY, TOO. I COULDN'T EVEN SLEEP LAST NIGHT. EXCITED.
WELL THEN, MAYBE YOU CAN CATCH SOME REST WHILE YOU'RE WAITING FOR ME.
SORRY?
I'M HANDLING THIS ONE ALONE, TOBY.
WHAT--WHAT ARE YOU TALKING ABOUT? THAT'S NOT THE DEAL. THAT'S NOT--THAT'S NOT THE ASSIGNMENT.
WE GO IN TOGETHER, I DO THE TALKING. THAT'S HOW THIS WORKS, REMEMBER?
NOT THIS TIME.
BUT--YOU CAN'T JUST GO IN THERE ALONE. WHAT ABOUT PROTOCOL? WE HAVE TO MONITOR EACH OTHER EVERY--
THAT'S WHY YOU GET TO LISTEN IN ON THIS.
NO ARGUMENTS.

HELLO?

ARE YOU COLLEEN?
YES, HI--
I'M LAUREN. I'M ANTHONY'S-- I DON'T KNOW, HIS ASSISTANT, I SUPPOSE.

THANK YOU FOR LETTING ME SEE HIM.
WELL, I'LL ADMIT I HAD SOME RESERVATIONS. BUT... HE DOESN'T GET MUCH COMPANY THESE DAYS. BESIDES ME, I MEAN--
SINCE HIS WIFE PASSED.

HE'S DOWNSTAIRS.
I SHOULD WARN YOU...IF HE'S WATCHING--WELL--IF HE'S WATCHING PORNOGRAPHY, PLEASE DON'T BE OFFENDED.
IT'S PART OF AN EXPERIMENT, TRYING TO TEST CERTAIN CHEMICAL RESPONSES IN THE CLONE BRAINS.
I UNDERSTAND.

PROFESSOR DUNN?

PROFESSOR DUNN?
YES?

JESUS, YOU SCARED--
I'M SORRY. I MEANT TO POSITION MYSELF IN FRONT OF YOU. I MIXED UP THE NUMBERS.

HERE. THIS ONE. THAT'S BETTER. I APOLOGIZE AGAIN.
FINE. FINE. JUST, PLEASE-- STOP DOING THAT. IT'S VERY--

1952.
IT'S UNSETTLING IS WHAT IT IS.

NEVER TOOK YOU FOR A SPIRITUALIST, EMIL.
I JUST THINK THERE ARE BETTER APPLICATIONS--
WE'RE TALKING ABOUT LIVING FOREVER HERE!
YOU'RE TALKING ABOUT TURNING YOUR CONSCIOUSNESS INTO WAVEFORMS. AT THAT POINT, IT'S NOT EVEN *YOU* ANYMORE. IT'S A COPY.
THEN HOISTING IT ONTO SOME CLONE FORM OVER AND OVER--
WE'VE DISCUSSED THIS--THE TRANSFER PROCESS DOESN'T COPY, IT BREAKS IT DOWN TO A MANAGEABLE BASE STRUCTURE AND--
IT'S INHUMAN!

SAYS THE BLOKE BUILDING A MIND-CONTROL HELMET.
AND IF ONLY I COULD GET IT TO WORK RIGHT NOW! YOU CAN'T ACTUALLY BE UNAWARE OF THE MORAL AND ETHICAL RAMIFICATIONS OF THIS. YOU CAN'T ***POSSIBLY*** BE SO DENSE, ANTHONY!

YOU KNOW WHAT I IMAGINE WILL SOLVE THIS ARGUMENT?
...HAVING A DRINK?
HAVING A DRINK.
THE MAN WHO WASN'T THERE...
NICK SPENCER: WRITER CAFU: PENCILLER BIT: INKER SANTIAGO ARCAS: COLORIST (Main Sequence)
HOWARD CHAYKIN: ARTIST JESUS ABURTOV: COLORIST (NoMan Sequence) SWANDS: LETTERER

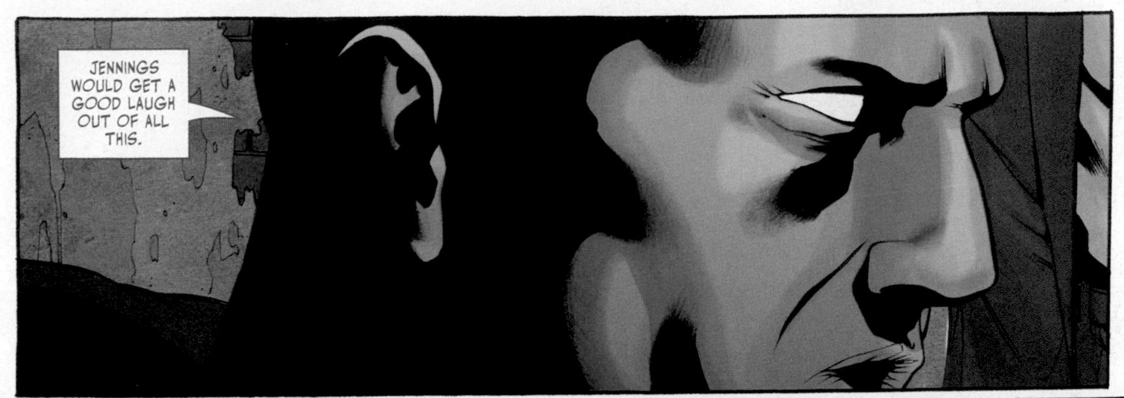
JENNINGS WOULD GET A GOOD LAUGH OUT OF ALL THIS.

WELL, THAT'S ACTUALLY PART OF THE REASON I'M HERE. T.H.U.N.D.E.R. HAS ASKED ME--
YOU'RE WITH *T.H.U.N.D.E.R.?*
SIR?

WHERE IS THE GIRL? I TOLD HER NOT TO LET ANY OF YOU COME--
SIR, PLEASE, I KNOW THIS MUST BE DIFFICULT FOR YOU, BUT... I JUST NEED A MOMENT.

PROFESSOR--
--DO YOU RECOGNIZE ME?

1967.
AND THIS IS WHY I LIKE SPIDER BETTER. AT LEAST THOSE GUYS CAN FIGHT WORTH A DAMN.
LEN, ARE YOU ALL RIGHT?
HM? OH, YEAH... YEAH, FINE.
DON'T SUPPOSE YOU GOT ONE OF THOSE BODIES YOU COULD LEND ME, HUH, DOC?

YOU SERVED ALONGSIDE THE ORIGINAL DYNAMO AND LIGHTNING. YOU'RE THE LAST OF THAT FIRST WAVE THAT REMAINS. PEOPLE LIKE MYSELF--WE ALL LOOK UP TO YOU, YOU KNOW.
THINGS AT T.H.U.N.D.E.R.--WELL, I DON'T KNOW IF IT WAS EVER--BUT THINGS ARE... MORE DIFFICULT NOW.
AND I THINK YOU KNOW I WOULDN'T BE HERE UNLESS THE SITUATION WAS EXTREMELY DIRE.
RAVEN--THE SAME RAVEN YOU SERVED WITH--HAS BEEN ABDUCTED BY A SPIDER TERROR CELL.
MY PARTNER AND I HAVE BEEN CHARGED WITH PUTTING TOGETHER A GROUP OF AGENTS TO STAGE AN EXTRACTION. AND MY SUPERIORS BELIEVE YOU SHOULD BE A PART OF THAT EFFORT.
BUT I'M NOT ASKING YOU TO DO THIS FOR THEM, SIR--I'M ASKING FOR RAVEN.
I'M ASKING ON BEHALF OF YOUR FRIEND.

1969.
EASY, DAN!
EASY MY ASS! HE ALMOST LET KITTEN DIE UP THERE--THE OLD FREAK IS LOSING IT!
HEY! HEY! YOU WANT CHAIN OF COMMAND TO FIND OUT YOU TOOK A SWING AT AN AGENT? GET THE HELL OUT OF HERE OR I'LL MAKE SURE IT HAPPENS. NOW.
I'M SORRY TO HAVE DRAGGED YOU INTO THAT, CRAIG. RESCUING HER CONFLICTED WITH THE MISSION OBJECTIVE--
THAT'S NOT THE RIGHT ANSWER, AND YOU KNOW IT.
I UNDERSTAND THAT SAVING A HUMAN LIFE IS MORE IMPORTANT.
BUT AS THESE TRANSFERS CONTINUE, EMOTIONAL RESPONSES SUCH AS EMPATHY...THEY SIMPLY DON'T COME AS QUICKLY AS THEY ONCE DID. THEY NO LONGER COME REFLEXIVELY.
LOOK, ANTHONY... YOU KNOW I'M YOUR FRIEND. BUT WHAT YOU'RE SAYING--IS THAT EVEN BEING HUMAN ANYMORE?
DON'T TAKE THIS THE WRONG WAY, BUT--
--YOU'VE ALREADY LIVED LONGER THAN ANY OF US EVER COULD.
IF YOU'RE REALLY STARTING TO LOSE WHAT MADE YOU YOU IN THE FIRST PLACE--
--WOULD IT BE SO BAD TO GIVE UP THE GHOST?

I AM SORRY FOR RAVEN, BUT I CAN BE OF NO ASSISTANCE, I'M AFRAID.
IS THIS THE INVISIBILITY CLOAK? AMAZING.

MY WIFE ALWAYS HATED IT. I'D FORGET I'D HAVE IT ON AND I WOULD FRIGHTEN HER.
I CAN IMAGINE THAT WOULD CAUSE SOME PROBLEMS.

SHE USED TO NAME THE CLONE BODIES. WHEN I WASN'T USING THEM.
THAT ONE OVER THERE SHE CALLED SYLVESTER. SO WHEN SHE WAS ANNOYED WITH ME, SHE'D LOOK AT ME IF I WAS USING IT AND SAY "BRING BACK SYLVESTER."
THAT'S WHEN I REALLY KNEW I WAS IN FOR IT.

DO YOU REMEMBER WHAT HAPPENED TO HER, PROFESSOR DUNN?

1973.

NO.
FINE.
LOOK, I GET THAT YOU DON'T WANT TO BE A PART OF THIS ANYMORE, SIR. I KNOW HOW MUCH YOU'VE GIVEN, AND HOW MUCH IT HURT YOU WHEN... IT ALL ENDED. AND I KNOW YOU JUST WANT TO BE LEFT ALONE NOW. I DO.
BUT UNFORTUNATELY, THAT'S JUST NOT AN OPTION ANYMORE.
WHAT I'M ABOUT TO TELL YOU IS FOR US ONLY, SIR--AND YOU KNOW WHY.
WHAT I'M ABOUT TO TELL YOU--YOU'LL UNDERSTAND WHY YOU HAVE TO COME BACK.
WAIT--WHAT HAPPENED TO THE AUDIO?!

1973.
PROFESSOR DUNN, DO YOU UNDERSTAND WHY YOU'RE HERE?
ACCORDING TO YOUR LETTER, YOU ARE TERMINATING MY SERVICE HERE WITH T.H.U.N.D.E.R., EFFECTIVE IMMEDIATELY.

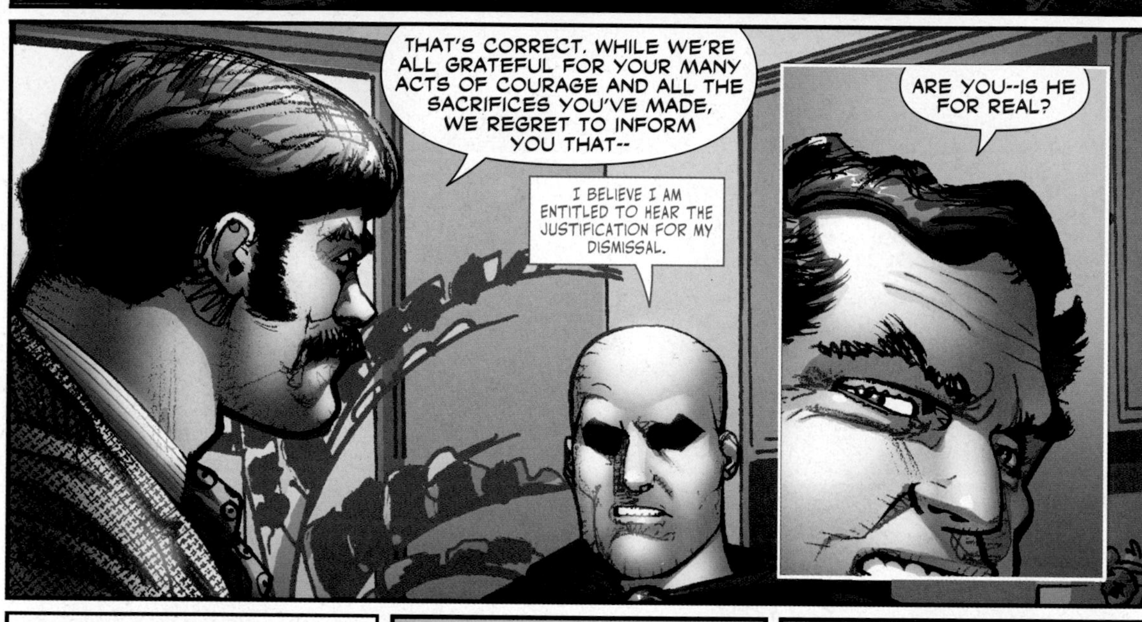
THAT'S CORRECT. WHILE WE'RE ALL GRATEFUL FOR YOUR MANY ACTS OF COURAGE AND ALL THE SACRIFICES YOU'VE MADE, WE REGRET TO INFORM YOU THAT--
I BELIEVE I AM ENTITLED TO HEAR THE JUSTIFICATION FOR MY DISMISSAL.
ARE YOU--IS HE FOR REAL?

FOR GOD'S SAKE, MAN, DO YOU EVEN--DO YOU EVEN KNOW WHAT HAPPENED TO YOUR WIFE?! YOU--YOU LET HER HANG HERSELF RIGHT IN FRONT OF YOU! SCOTLAND YARD IS TALKING ABOUT CHARGING YOU WITH CRIMINAL NEGLIGIENCE!

WHAT'S WRONG WITH HIM NOW?
...I DON'T THINK HE'S IN THERE ANYMORE...

COME ON--
COME ON--
HEY, HEY! OPEN UP! YOU LOST THE AUDIO!
BANG
BANG
OH. I, UH-- THIS THING ISN'T--
WE'RE READY.
LET'S GO.
OH MY GOD. HE REALLY IS BLUE.

SRI LANKA.
NOW.
SO NOW THAT LIGHTNING'S PINCHED THE POWER GRID, THIS SHOULD BE EASY, RIGHT?
NoMAN PUTS ON THE NO-SEE-ME HOODIE AND JUST WALKS IN THERE TO PICK UP RAVEN?
"THAT IS THE PLAN, YES."

WELL I JUST CAN'T WAIT TO SEE HOW THIS GOES WRONG.

OKAY, THE HELL IF I KNOW WHAT HAPPENED--BUT IT'S ALL BACK ONLINE NOW.
YOU KNOW HOW IT IS--EVERYTHING IN THIS PLACE IS LIKE FIFTY YEARS OLD. NONE OF THIS JUNK WORKS.
HMMPH. SPIDER-GOING-OUT-OF-BUSINESS SALE. FIGURES.
JACOBSON TOOK OFF. DO A SHOT WITH ME.
KLNK
SO IT'S JUST US THEN? I MEAN, BESIDES THE HUSK UPSTAIRS--
MMM.

HEY, ANTHONY.

DON'T WORRY, THEY DON'T HAVE ANY CAMERAS IN HERE.

HOW DID YOU KNOW?
DOESN'T MATTER.
GOOD TO SEE YOU AGAIN, OLD FELLA.

THESE NEW SPIDER SOLDIERS-- THEY'RE ALL SO... YOUNG.
NO KIDDING. THAT'S THE FIRST THING I SAID, TOO. SOME OF 'EM ARE STILL IN COLLEGE. RUNNING A TERRORIST ORGANIZATION OUT OF THEIR DORM ROOMS.
NOT EXACTLY LIKE THE OLD DAYS.

ARE YOU HURT?
WORSE THAN THAT. BUT THEY'RE KEEPING ME ALIVE.
AND YOU AND I BOTH KNOW WHY.

THE BODIES.

I NEVER DID SAY I WAS SORRY. TO YOU. I ALWAYS REGRETTED THAT.

WHAT'S DONE IS DONE.
"THE PATH TO A TRULY SAFER TOMORROW IS ALWAYS THE RIGHTEOUS ONE--"
JESUS. COULD THEY HAVE ***BEEN*** MORE SANCTIMONIOUS BASTARDS?
WE'RE GONNA GET WHAT WE DESERVE HERE. THESE KIDS ARE BETTER THAN US. THEY'RE GONNA BURN IT ALL TO THE GROUND.
I DOUBT THAT. I DIDN'T COME BACK JUST TO WATCH ALL WE WORKED FOR END LIKE THIS.

EH, LIKE I SAID, DOESN'T MATTER--

KZZZZT
THEY ALREADY KNEW YOU WERE COMING.
JESUS... LOOK AT HIM. MAKES YOUR STOMACH KIND OF CURL UP, DOESN'T IT?
ONE GUY'S PATHOLOGICAL NEED NOT TO DIE TURNS HIM INTO A MEMBER OF *THE BLUE MAN GROUP*. SAD.
YOU CAN'T KILL HIM, YOU KNOW. HE'S GOT IT SET UP NOW SO THAT HIS MIND JUST IMMEDIATELY MOVES OVER TO ANOTHER BODY ONCE THE HEART STOPS PUMPING BLOOD TO THE BRAIN. HE WANTED TO PREVENT HIMSELF FROM BEING ABLE TO COMMIT SUICIDE.
CAN I, JUST THIS ONCE?
BE MY GUEST.
YOU THINK WE DON'T ALREADY KNOW THAT?!?
THAT'S WHAT HAPPENS WHEN YOU START TALKING DOWN TO US.
WE GOT A BODY NOW. WHEN JACOBSON GETS BACK HERE, TIME FOR THE NUMBERS. UNDERSTOOD?
THERE'S NO USE PUTTING UP A FIGHT ANYMORE. REMEMBER--

"WE HAVE A MAN ON THE INSIDE."

Cover by **Ethan Van Sciver**, **Scott Hanna** & **Hi-Fi**, after **Wally Wood** & **Dan Adkins**

ETHAN
V 2010

HELLO, AND WELCOME TO T.H.U.N.D.E.R. AGENT ORIENTATION!

I AM DOCTOR VAANI NANDAKUMAR, AND ON BEHALF OF THE ENTIRE HIGHER UNITED NATIONS--
--I MUST BEGIN BY TELLING YOU THAT IT IS AN HONOR AND A PRIVILEGE TO HAVE YOU WITH US TODAY!

YOUR WILLINGNESS TO SERVE HUMANITY SELFLESSLY AND IN THE FACE OF GREAT DANGER DOES NOT GO UNNOTICED BY US--
--AND OUR JOB IS TO MAKE SURE YOU HAVE ALL THE TOOLS AND SUPPORT NECESSARY TO HELP YOU CARRY OUT YOUR MISSION IN A SAFE AND RESPONSIBLE MANNER.
YOUR SERVICE CARRIES ON A GRAND TRADITION.
"SINCE 1967, WITH THE USE OF EQUIPMENT INVENTED AND DESIGNED BY THE LEGENDARY RESEARCH TEAM OF EMIL JENNINGS AND ANTHONY DUNN--
"--THE HIGHER UNITED NATIONS DEFENSE ENFORCEMENT RESERVES HAVE BEEN TASKED WITH COUNTERING GLOBAL THREATS DEEMED TOO VOLATILE AND TIME-SENSITIVE IN NATURE FOR TRADITIONAL ENGAGEMENT VIA THE SECURITY COUNCIL.
"THOSE ORIGINAL AGENTS SAVED THE WORLD COUNTLESS TIMES FROM GRAVE THREATS OF ALL DIFFERENT KINDS--

"AND THEY WERE BUT THE FIRST OF MANY.
"FOR THE LAST FOUR-PLUS DECADES, THE T.H.U.N.D.E.R. AGENTS PROGRAM HAS BEEN A BEACON OF HOPE IN TIMES OF CRISIS, THE PROTECTOR OF PEACE AND PROSPERITY ALL ACROSS THE GLOBE.

"WHILE THE MEN AND WOMEN WHO WEAR THESE UNIFORMS MIGHT CHANGE, THEY ALL STAND FOR ONE SINGULAR PURPOSE, ALL PROTECTING THE SAME TRADITION, THE SAME LEGACY.
"AND NOW THE RESPONSIBILITY OF PRESERVING THAT GREAT LEGACY FALLS ON YOU."

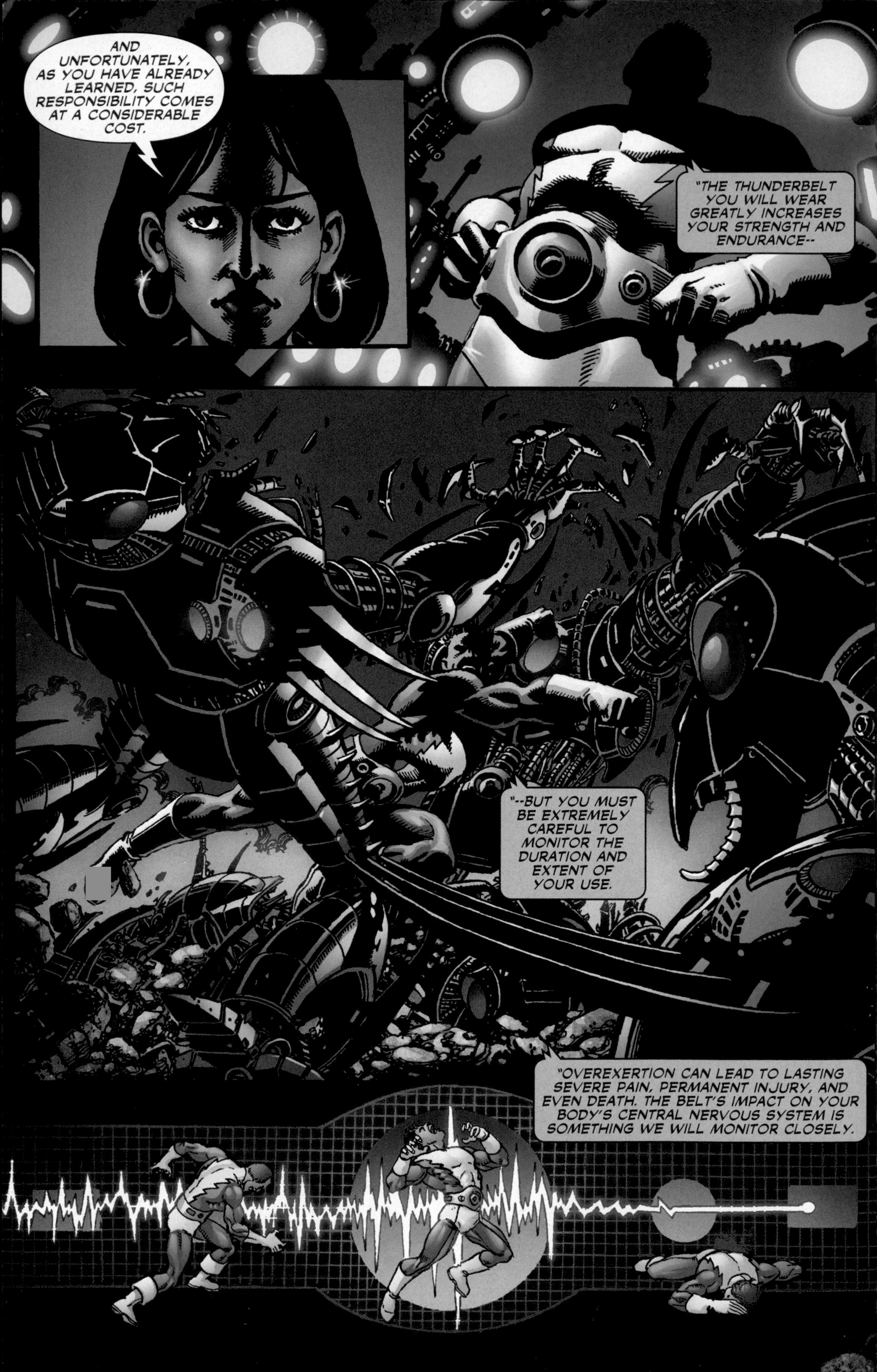
AND UNFORTUNATELY, AS YOU HAVE ALREADY LEARNED, SUCH RESPONSIBILITY COMES AT A CONSIDERABLE COST.
"THE THUNDERBELT YOU WILL WEAR GREATLY INCREASES YOUR STRENGTH AND ENDURANCE--
"--BUT YOU MUST BE EXTREMELY CAREFUL TO MONITOR THE DURATION AND EXTENT OF YOUR USE.
"OVEREXERTION CAN LEAD TO LASTING SEVERE PAIN, PERMANENT INJURY, AND EVEN DEATH. THE BELT'S IMPACT ON YOUR BODY'S CENTRAL NERVOUS SYSTEM IS SOMETHING WE WILL MONITOR CLOSELY.

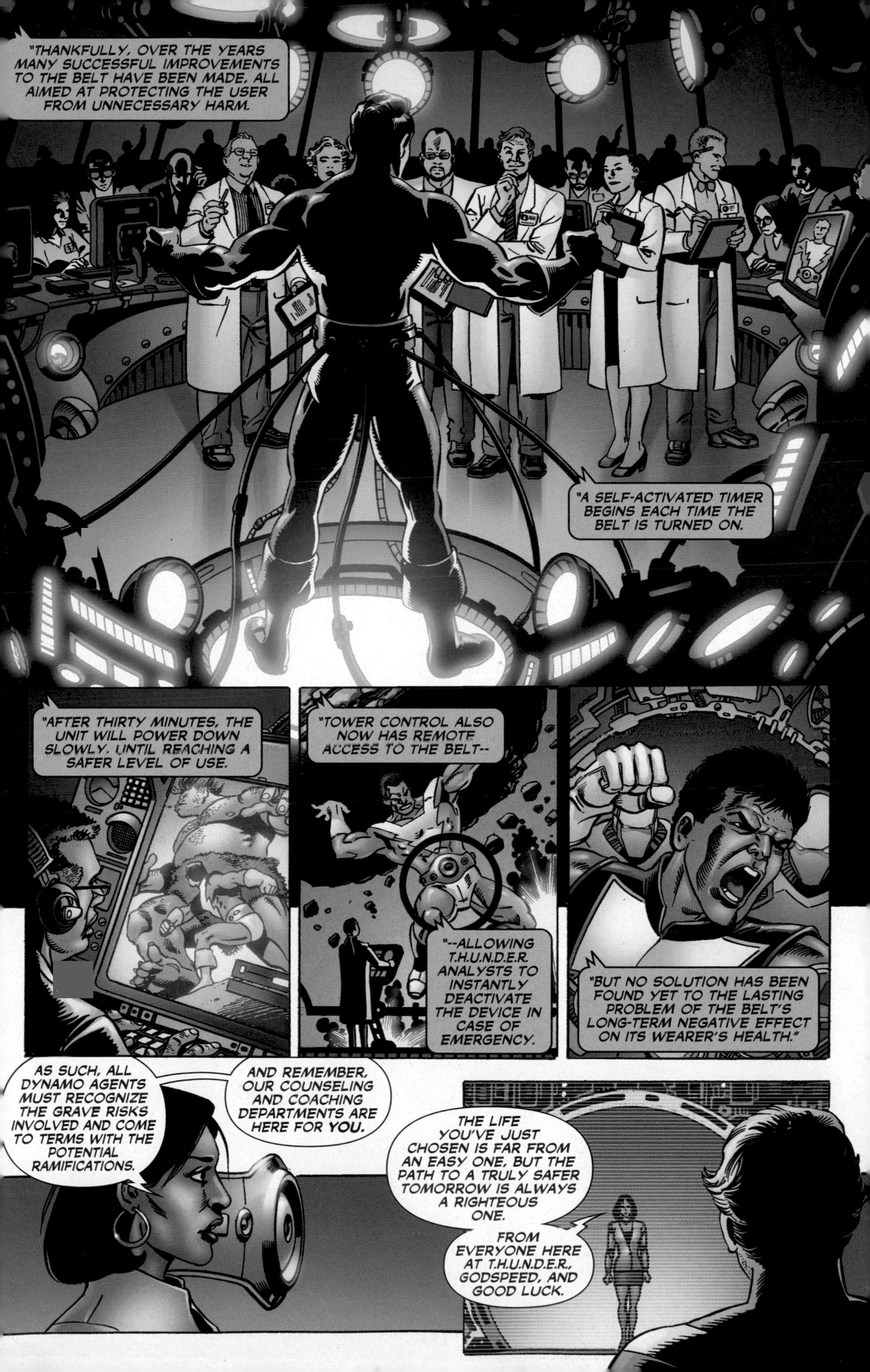
"THANKFULLY, OVER THE YEARS MANY SUCCESSFUL IMPROVEMENTS TO THE BELT HAVE BEEN MADE, ALL AIMED AT PROTECTING THE USER FROM UNNECESSARY HARM.
"A SELF-ACTIVATED TIMER BEGINS EACH TIME THE BELT IS TURNED ON.
"AFTER THIRTY MINUTES, THE UNIT WILL POWER DOWN SLOWLY, UNTIL REACHING A SAFER LEVEL OF USE.
"TOWER CONTROL ALSO NOW HAS REMOTE ACCESS TO THE BELT--
"--ALLOWING T.H.U.N.D.E.R. ANALYSTS TO INSTANTLY DEACTIVATE THE DEVICE IN CASE OF EMERGENCY.
"BUT NO SOLUTION HAS BEEN FOUND YET TO THE LASTING PROBLEM OF THE BELT'S LONG-TERM NEGATIVE EFFECT ON ITS WEARER'S HEALTH."
AS SUCH, ALL DYNAMO AGENTS MUST RECOGNIZE THE GRAVE RISKS INVOLVED AND COME TO TERMS WITH THE POTENTIAL RAMIFICATIONS.
AND REMEMBER, OUR COUNSELING AND COACHING DEPARTMENTS ARE HERE FOR YOU.
THE LIFE YOU'VE JUST CHOSEN IS FAR FROM AN EASY ONE, BUT THE PATH TO A TRULY SAFER TOMORROW IS ALWAYS A RIGHTEOUS ONE.
FROM EVERYONE HERE AT T.H.U.N.D.E.R., GODSPEED, AND GOOD LUCK.

NICK SPENCER: WRITER CAFU: PENCILLER BIT: INKER SANTIAGO ARCAS: COLORIST [Main Sequence]
GEORGE PÉREZ: PENCILLER SCOTT KOBLISH & PÉREZ: INKERS BLOND: COLORIST [Dynamo Sequence] SWANDS: LETTERER

AND DON'T EVEN THINK ABOUT COMING BACK!

WELL, ERIC, I WAS GOING TO START OFF BUYING YOU A DRINK--SO THERE WENT THAT.

WHO THE HELL ARE YOU?
MY NAME IS TOBY HENSTON, THIS IS MY ASSOCIATE, COLLEEN FRANKLIN. WE WORK FOR THE HIGHER UNITED NATIONS.

THE HIGHER UNITED NATIONS? THEY STILL TELLIN' THAT JOKE?
IS HE--?

YES. YES, HE IS. THE NEW DYNAMO IS PUBLICLY URINATING OUTSIDE A BAR IN TUSCALOOSA. THAT IS HAPPENING.
THE NEW WHAT?

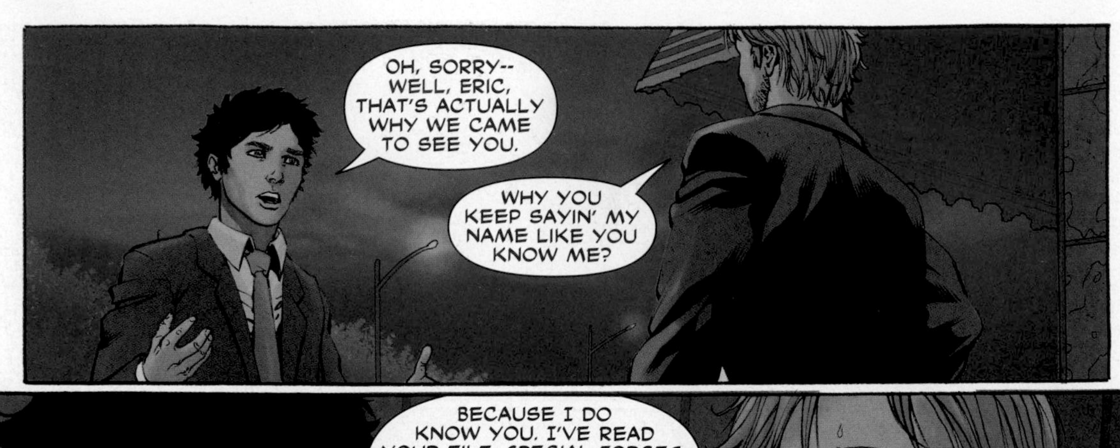
OH, SORRY-- WELL, ERIC, THAT'S ACTUALLY WHY WE CAME TO SEE YOU.
WHY YOU KEEP SAYIN' MY NAME LIKE YOU KNOW ME?

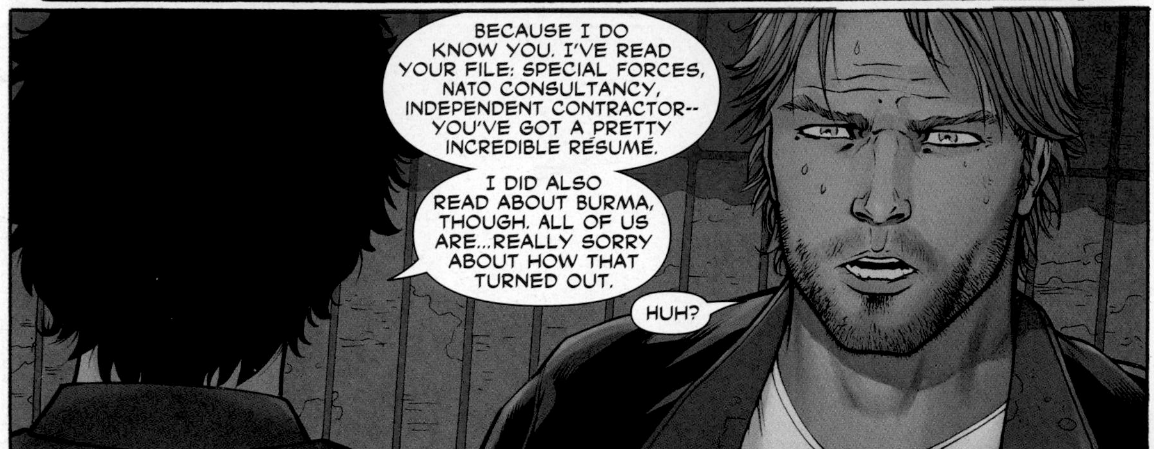
BECAUSE I DO KNOW YOU. I'VE READ YOUR FILE: SPECIAL FORCES, NATO CONSULTANCY, INDEPENDENT CONTRACTOR-- YOU'VE GOT A PRETTY INCREDIBLE RESUMÉ.
I DID ALSO READ ABOUT BURMA, THOUGH. ALL OF US ARE...REALLY SORRY ABOUT HOW THAT TURNED OUT.
HUH?

IT'S JUST-- I KNOW THAT MUST'VE BEEN PRETTY BAD.
STILL GOT PAID, DIDN'T I?

RIGHT.
WELL, THERE YA GO THEN.

OKAY, WELL--IF YOU'RE INTERESTED--
PLEASE JUST SHUT YOUR DAMN MOUTH AND LET THE PRETTY ONE TELL ME WHAT THE JOB IS.

SRI LANKA.
NOW.
NO! NO, NO-NO! DAMN IT!
WHAT HAPPENED?
DUNN-- NOMAN-- HE'S OFFLINE.
HOW? YOU SAID THEY DIDN'T KNOW HE WAS BACK--
YEAH, WELL, APPARENTLY THEY DID.
SO WHAT DO WE DO NOW?
I DON'T KNOW! I DON'T KNOW! JESUS, WHAT THE HELL ARE YOU EVEN DOING HERE? WHY IS THE SALESMAN COMING OUT ON FIELD MISSIONS NOW?
THEY--THEY THOUGHT IT MIGHT HAVE A CALMING EFFECT ON THE NEW AGENTS...
YEAH, YOU'RE A REAL PORT IN A STORM, AREN'T YOU, MATE?

DYNAMO! GET OVER HERE--

--YOU'RE UP.

WHAT'S THE PLAN?
THERE IS NO PLAN. GET IN THERE AND START BEATING THE HELL OUT OF EVERYTHING IN SIGHT. DON'T COME OUT WITHOUT OUR ASSETS.

I LIKE HOW YOU WORK, SWEETHEART.

T.H.U.N.D.E.R. TOWER.
NOW.
PERIMETER PATROL 1940, ALL NORMAL.
YOU REALLY DIDN'T LIKE IT?

IT DOESN'T MAKE ANY SENSE.
WHAT DOESN'T MAKE SENSE? SHE'S BECOMING THE SWAN QUEEN. HOW DO YOU NOT GET THIS?!

I JUST DIDN'T *CARE*, YOU KNOW? I WANTED TO, I REALLY DID, BUT--
OH, HELL--

OKAY, THE GIRL FROM *THAT '70S SHOW* WAS HOT, I'LL GIVE YOU THAT--
THAT IS NOT GOOD. THAT IS ***REALLY*** NOT GOOD.

WE NEED DIRECTOR KEANE. ***NOW.***

TUSCALOOSA, ALABAMA.
THEN.
YOU STRIKE ME AS A SERIOUS MAN, SO I'LL BE DIRECT.
WE'RE HERE TO OFFER YOU A SPOT IN THE RANKS OF THE T.H.U.N.D.E.R. AGENTS. TO BECOME THE NEW DYNAMO, SPECIFICALLY.
YOUR BACKGROUND AND SKILL SET, IN PARTICULAR, MAKE YOU A STRONG FIT FOR THE PROGRAM. THE REST IS COMPLICATED, BUT... LOOK--
--THIS IS A CHANCE TO BE A HERO. A CHANCE TO DO GREAT THINGS AND MAKE THE WORLD A BETTER PLACE.
IT'S ALSO A VERY DANGEROUS JOB. NOT JUST BECAUSE OF THE THREATS YOU'LL FACE--AND TRUST ME, THEY ARE *SEVERE*--
--BUT ALSO BECAUSE OF THE EQUIPMENT YOU'LL WEAR. THE THUNDERBELT GRANTS METAHUMAN-LEVEL STRENGTH AND ENDURANCE, BUT IT COMES AT A HEAVY COST.
THE TRUTH IS--AND I WANT TO BE UPFRONT ABOUT THIS--
--FOR T.H.U.N.D.E.R. AGENTS OVER THE LAST FOUR DECADES, AVERAGE TENURE OF SERVICE IS LESS THAN A YEAR, AND THE SURVIVAL RATE IS ESSENTIALLY *ZERO.*

SO WHAT'S THE MONEY LIKE?
I'M SORRY, DID YOU CATCH THAT LAST PART ABOUT THE SURVIVAL RATE?
MOST OF MY JOBS, YOU THINK THEY TELL ME I'M COMIN' BACK? I DON'T NEED NO DAMN SERMON. WHAT'S THE *MONEY* LIKE?
WELL, T.H.U.N.D.E.R. DOES OFFER A SOLID COMPENSATION PACKAGE FOR YOU AND YOUR ESTATE, BUT--
WHAT'S YOUR NAME, HONEY?
UM, HEY, YOU KNOW, THERE'S THIS WILDE QUOTE THAT REMINDS ME OF YOU--
YEAH, WHAT I THOUGHT. I COST A LOT MORE'N GOVERNMENT MONEY CAN AFFORD TO PAY--
--BUT MAYBE *YOU* COULD THROW IN A LITTLE EXTRA.

OKAY, THAT'S IT. TO HELL WITH THIS. WE'RE DONE HERE. COME ON, COLLEEN--
YOU'RE A PIECE OF $&@#, YOU KNOW THAT? WHAT HAPPENED IN BURMA, YOU LETTING THOSE KIDS DIE LIKE THAT, YOU DON'T DESERVE TO BE A HERO. YOU DON'T DESERVE TO BE ***BREATHING,*** QUITE FRANKLY.
THE IDEA OF GIVING A GUY LIKE YOU A SECOND CHANCE--EVEN ONE AS MESSED UP AS THIS--MAKES ME SICK.
I CAN'T RESCIND THE OFFER. THAT'S NOT MY CALL TO MAKE.
BUT I'M GONNA GO BACK TO MY OFFICE AND DO EVERYTHING I CAN TO MAKE SURE THIS DOESN'T HAPPEN, ***DANIEL*** OR ***NO DANIEL.*** HELL--

--IF THEY HIRE YOU, I'LL QUIT MYSELF.

HEY. THAT WAS... THAT WAS *UNEXPECTED.*
YEAH?

BUT YOU SHOULDN'T HAVE DONE THAT. I COULD'VE BROKEN HIS NECK FOUR DIFFERENT WAYS IF I'D WANTED TO. NOT THAT I DON'T APPRECIATE IT, BUT--
--WELL... THERE'S GONNA BE HELL TO PAY FOR THIS. KEANE IS GOING TO KILL US FOR LOSING THE PROSPECT. YOU CAN'T JUST--
UM, HOLD ON, DO YOU THINK--DO YOU THINK I DID THAT TO BE--*CHIVALROUS?*

DO YOU THINK I *LIKE* YOU?

WHAT ARE YOU TALKING ABOUT?
COLLEEN, I GET YOU DON'T THINK MUCH OF ME, BUT HEY--AT LEAST RESPECT MY ABILITIES AS A SALESMAN! I KNOW HUMAN REACTIONS.

SEE? HERE HE COMES NOW.

I NEED TO SPEAK TO DIRECTOR KEANE RIGHT AWAY!
EXCUSE ME, YOU CAN'T JUST--

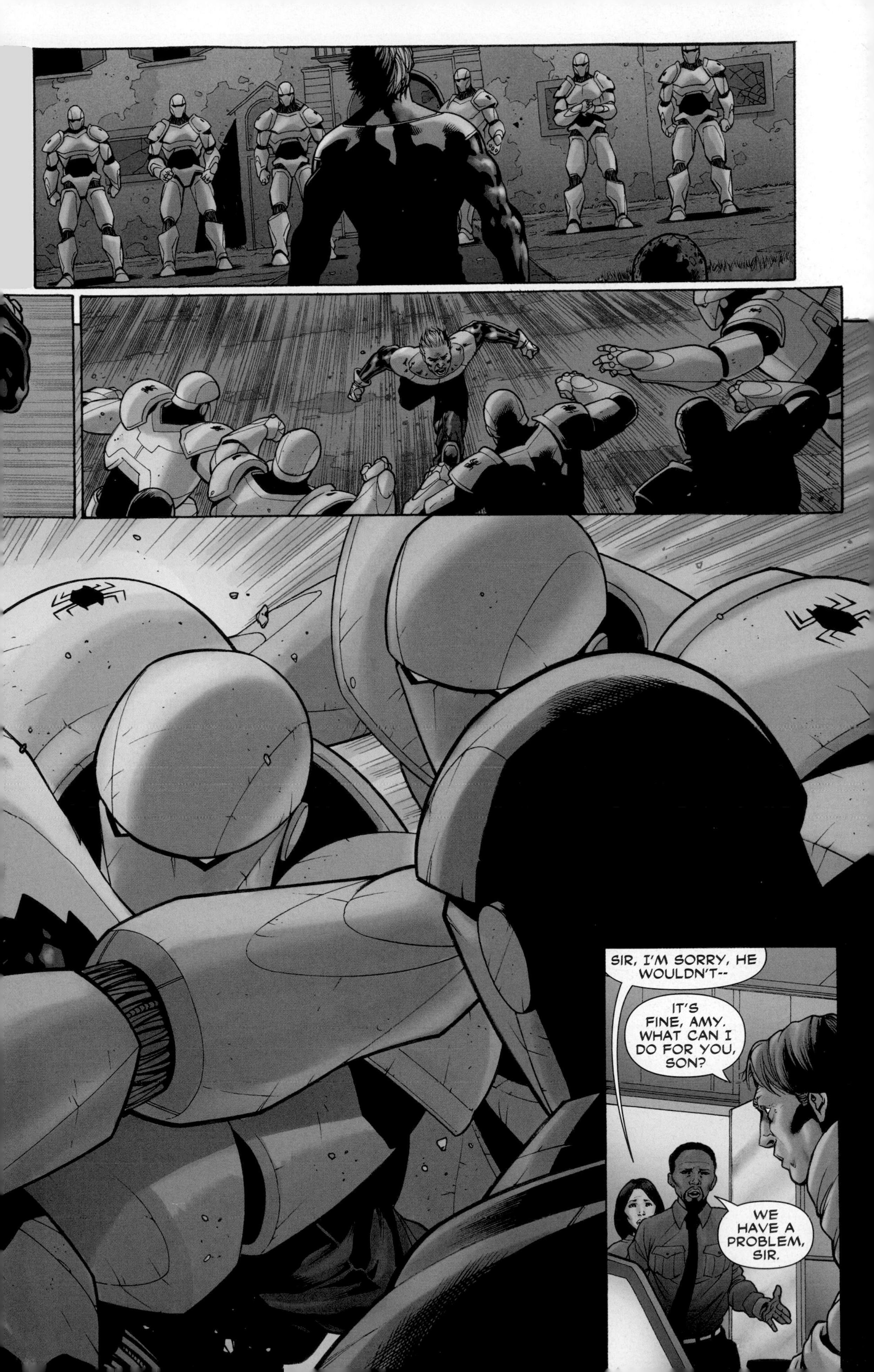
SIR, I'M SORRY, HE WOULDN'T--
IT'S FINE, AMY. WHAT CAN I DO FOR YOU, SON?
WE HAVE A PROBLEM, SIR.

KZZZRK
YOU'RE CERTAIN?
SIR, I WOULDN'T-- WELL, JUST SEE FOR YOURSELF, SIR--
CHOOM
ZZZAT

IT'S GONE, SIR.
"THE MENTHOR HELMET IS GONE!"
ERIC LINDAHL, THE T.H.U.N.D.E.R. AGENT CALLED DYNAMO...
SPIDER ONLY HAS A QUESTION:

WHY DID GOD HARDEN THE PHARAOH'S HEART?

Cover by **Francis Manapul** & **Brian Buccellato**,
after **Steve Ditko**, **Wally Wood** & **Dan Adkins**

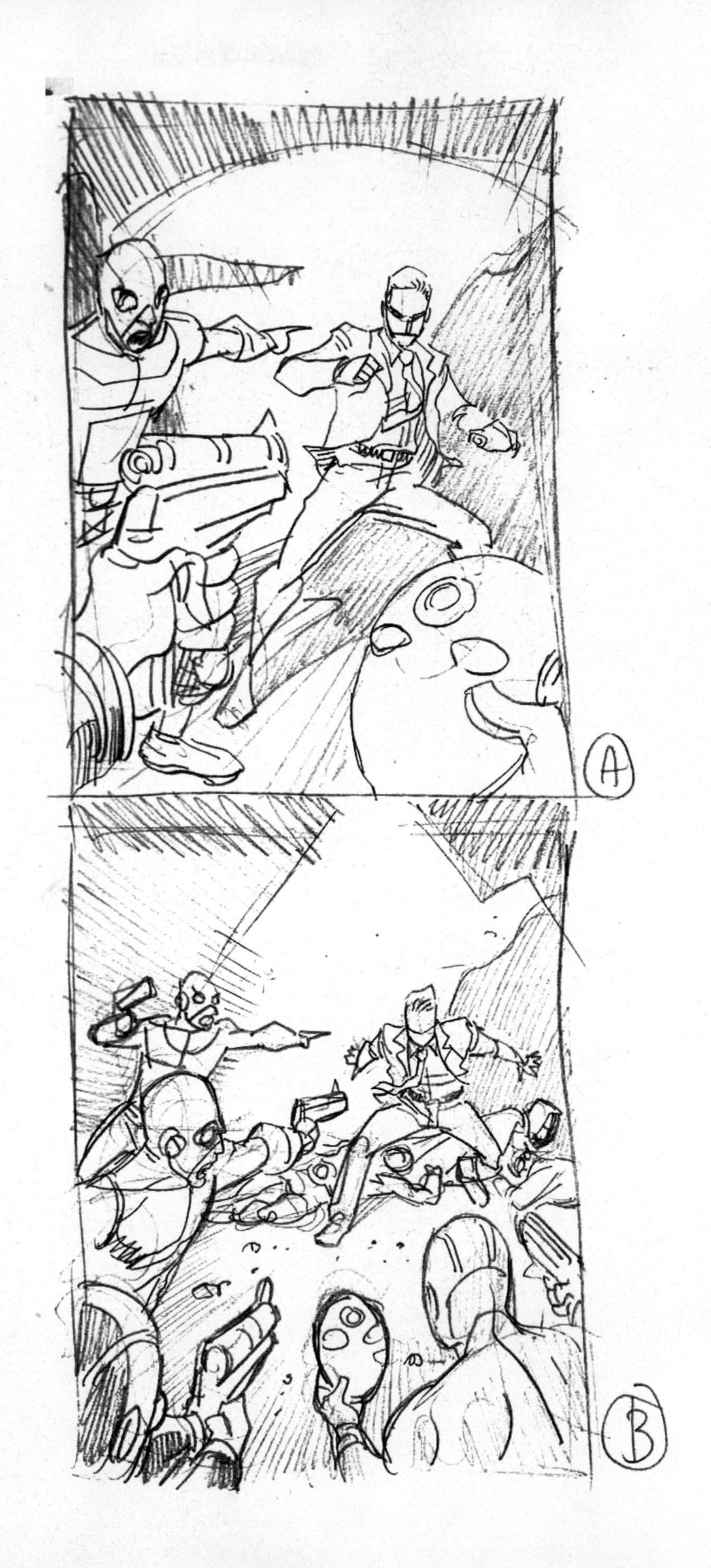
A
B

FIVE YEARS AGO.
YOU BOUGHT A TERRORIST ORGANIZATION?
I DID. HAVE YOU EVER HEARD OF SPIDER?
NO...
YEAH, ME EITHER. APPARENTLY THEY WERE BIG BACK IN THE '60s. JUST SOME CHEAP, TWO-BIT CROOK ENTERPRISE. BUT THEY HAVE A LOT OF GOOD EQUIPMENT, AND THEY'RE POSITIONED GLOBALLY.
LIKE... ON EBAY?
NOT QUITE EBAY.
WHAT DID YOU SPEND YOUR PART OF THE INHERITANCE ON, THEN?
DOESN'T MATTER, SHE STILL LEFT. FRASER, WAIT--WHAT EXACTLY DOES ONE DO WITH A TERRORIST ORGANIZATION?
EXACTLY WHAT MOM AND DAD TOLD US TO:
GO CHANGE THE WORLD.

THREE MONTHS LATER.
DO YOU KNOW WHY I ASKED ALL OF YOU HERE?
BECAUSE YOU'RE RICH, AND YOU LIKE TO FLY US NICE PLACES?

BECAUSE YOU'RE MY BEST FRIENDS. BECAUSE YOU'RE THE PEOPLE I CARE ABOUT THE MOST IN THIS LIFE. YOU'RE THE PEOPLE I TRUST.

WHEN JAMES AND I-- WHEN OUR PARENTS PASSED AWAY, WE FOUND OURSELVES WITH RESOURCES. AND A PURPOSE.
OUR FAMILY WAS NEVER RELIGIOUS. WASN'T UNTIL UNIVERSITY THAT I SPENT ANY TIME LOOKING AT A BIBLE, REALLY. BUT ONE DAY I WAS DOING JUST THAT, AND I CAME ACROSS THIS VERSE, I CAN NEVER FORGET--

"BUT I WILL HARDEN PHARAOH'S HEART, AND THOUGH I MULTIPLY MY SIGNS AND WONDERS IN EGYPT, HE WILL NOT LISTEN TO YOU. THEN I WILL LAY MY HAND ON EGYPT, WITH MIGHTY ACTS OF JUDGMENT--" ET CETERA, ET CETERA.

NOW, THIS IS THE STORY OF THE PLAGUES, WE ALL KNOW IT. GOD SENDS MOSES TO THE PHARAOH, DEMANDS HE FREES THE HEBREWS-- PLAGUES, PESTILENCE, AND FAMINE FROM THERE.
BUT WHY DID GOD HARDEN THE PHARAOH'S HEART? WHY WOULD HE-- OR HOW *COULD* HE--PUNISH EGYPT IF HE FIRST TAKES AWAY ITS LEADER'S FREE WILL?
OH, GREAT. FRASER'S FOUND RELIGION.

NO. YOU SEE, THAT'S EXACTLY MY POINT. THIS STORY HAS NOTHING TO DO WITH RELIGION. THIS IS ABOUT THE ILLUSION OF CHOICE. THIS IS ABOUT THE GAMES THESE FORCES PLAY WITH PEOPLE'S LIVES IN ORDER TO, WHAT? ACQUIRE. CONSUME. HOARD. DOMINATE. THAT'S ALL THIS IS. THESE HEADS OF STATE, AND THEIR PRETENSE OF POWER.
THIS IS ABOUT ALL THE OPPRESSION AND APARTHEID WE'VE ALL DEDICATED OUR LIVES TO DOING SOMETHING ABOUT FINALLY BEING EXPOSED FOR WHAT IT REALLY IS--
--THE FASCISM THAT'S BEEN HANDED DOWN THROUGH CHAINS OF CONTROL FROM THEIR IMAGINARY GODS ON DOWNWARD. A FALSE GAME OF SIDES WHERE NOTHING IS EVER REALLY LEFT TO CHANCE, WHERE NO FREE WILL EXISTS.
WE CAN BE THE ONES WHO END ALL THIS. YOU CAN SEE THE CRACKS EVERYWHERE--THE COLLAPSES IN THEIR FINANCIAL SYSTEMS AS THEIR GREED STARTS TO MAKE THEM EAT AWAY AT THEMSELVES--
--THEIR VALUES SPIRALING DOWNWARD EVEN AS THEY TRY TO TAKE MORE AND MORE FROM THOSE WITH LESS. THEY'RE SCARED, AND THEY'RE DESPERATE.
AND IN THEIR DESPERATION AND THEIR ARROGANCE, THEY BUILT SOMETHING. SOMETHING THAT--IF WE CAN REACH IT, IF WE CAN MAKE IT OURS--COULD ACTUALLY ***CHANGE*** ALL OF THIS.

I'M ASKING YOU TO STEP OUTSIDE ALL YOU KNOW. EVERYTHING I TELL YOU FROM HERE, IT WILL BE TERRIFYING. IT WILL SOUND INSANE. SPIDER, ACTS OF AGGRESSION, VIOLENT OVERTHROW OF ESTABLISHED SYSTEMS--IT WILL SOUND IMPOSSIBLE AND NAIVE. DANGEROUS.
IT WILL SOUND ANTIQUATED. LIKE RED ARMY FACTION LUNACY. IT WILL SOUND TERRIFYINGLY UNREALISTIC. BUT IF YOU KEEP LISTENING, YOU'LL RECOGNIZE WHAT ELSE IT SOUNDS LIKE--

--IT WILL SOUND LIKE THE TRUTH.

SO WHO WANTS TO HEAR MORE?

I DO.

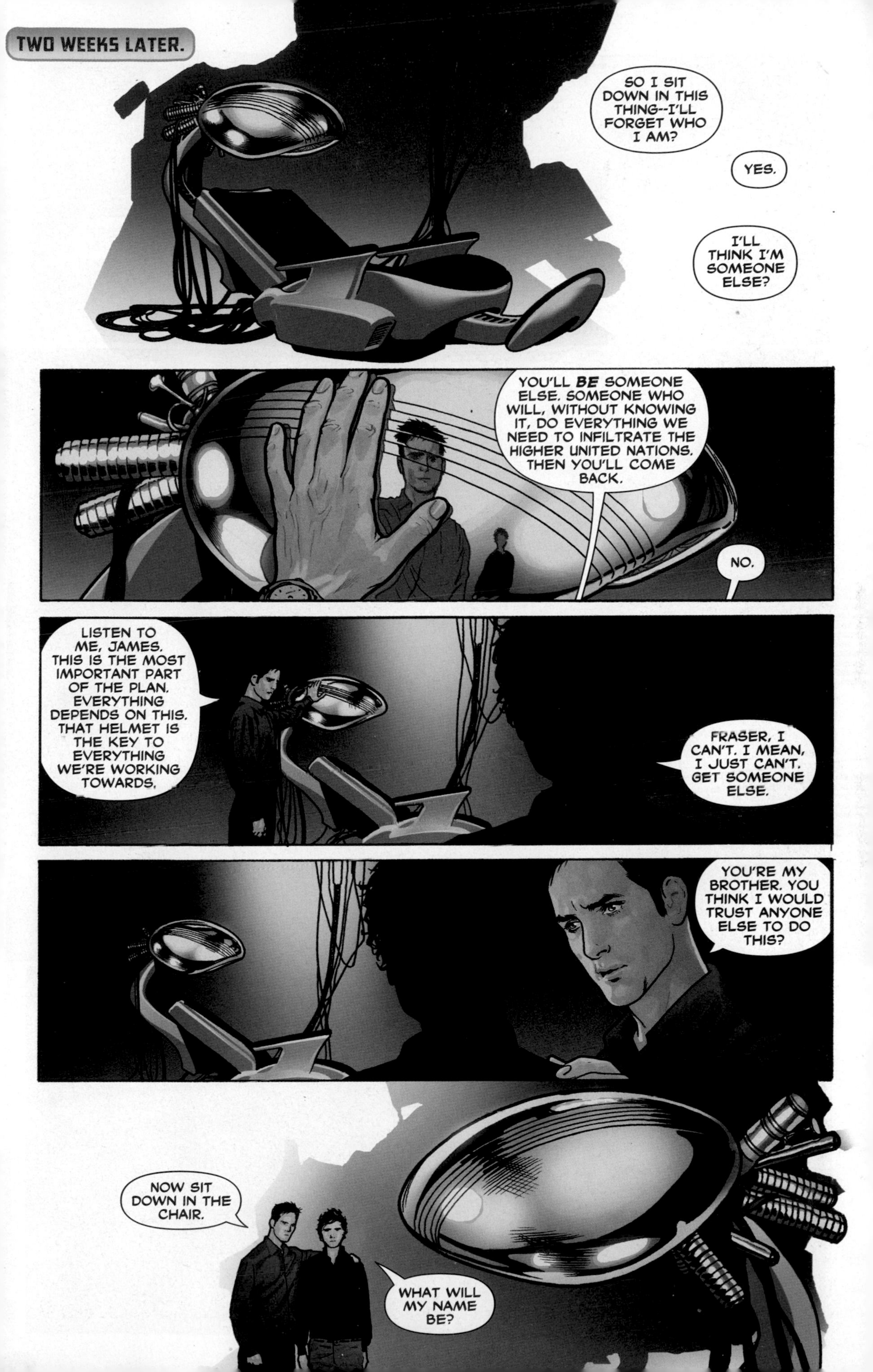
TWO WEEKS LATER.
SO I SIT DOWN IN THIS THING--I'LL FORGET WHO I AM?
YES.
I'LL THINK I'M SOMEONE ELSE?
YOU'LL BE SOMEONE ELSE. SOMEONE WHO WILL, WITHOUT KNOWING IT, DO EVERYTHING WE NEED TO INFILTRATE THE HIGHER UNITED NATIONS. THEN YOU'LL COME BACK.
NO.
LISTEN TO ME, JAMES. THIS IS THE MOST IMPORTANT PART OF THE PLAN. EVERYTHING DEPENDS ON THIS. THAT HELMET IS THE KEY TO EVERYTHING WE'RE WORKING TOWARDS.
FRASER, I CAN'T. I MEAN, I JUST CAN'T. GET SOMEONE ELSE.
YOU'RE MY BROTHER. YOU THINK I WOULD TRUST ANYONE ELSE TO DO THIS?
NOW SIT DOWN IN THE CHAIR.
WHAT WILL MY NAME BE?

NOW.
THERE HE IS!

JESUS CHRIST...
NEVER THE WHOLE TRUTH
NICK SPENCER: WRITER
CAFU: PENCILLER BIT: INKER SANTIAGO ARCAS: COLORIST [MAIN SEQUENCE]
RYAN SOOK: ARTIST [MENTHOR SEQUENCE] SWANDS: LETTERER

I DON'T GET IT. HE DOESN'T LOOK A DAY OLDER.
SO, KID--

"--YOU READY TO SEE BIG BROTHER?"
YEAH... OKAY, WELL THEN-- I'M JUST GONNA LEAVE YOU TWO ALONE...
...YOU'RE OKAY.
I'M OKAY.

LIGHTNING--

--I NEED YOU.
PLEASE, MISS--I CANNOT--

AT THIS POINT, I'VE LOST DYNAMO AND NoMAN. I CAN'T FIND ONE OF MY OPERATIVES. THIS IS GOING TO COME DOWN TO YOU AND ME.

I CANNOT.

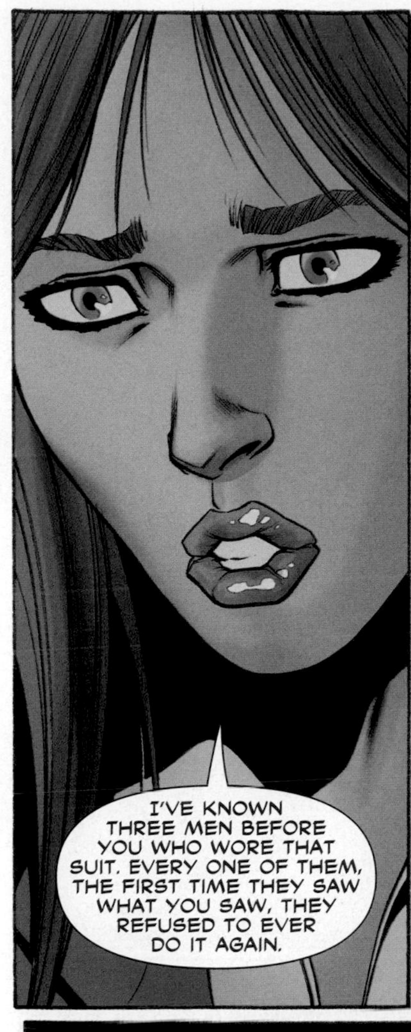
I'VE KNOWN THREE MEN BEFORE YOU WHO WORE THAT SUIT. EVERY ONE OF THEM, THE FIRST TIME THEY SAW WHAT YOU SAW, THEY REFUSED TO EVER DO IT AGAIN.

EVENTUALLY SOMEONE JUST POINTS AT WHOEVER IS IN TROUBLE, WHOEVER NEEDS OUR HELP, AND SAYS "YES, YOU KEEP DOING THIS, YOU WILL BE DIE. BUT IF YOU DON'T--"

"--THEY WILL."

WHETHER THAT'S A GOOD ENOUGH REASON FOR YOU TELLS ME ALL I'LL EVER NEED TO KNOW ABOUT WHETHER OR NOT YOU WERE THE *RIGHT* PERSON FOR THIS JOB.

WE'RE LEAVING IN TEN.

HOW DOES IT FEEL?
LIKE I'VE BEEN SUBLETTING MY FRONTAL LOBES, AND THEY LEFT A MESS.
WHEN DID YOU WAKE UP?
A GIRL WAS YELLING AT ME.

YOU NEVER CHANGE. GO GET SOME REST.
ARE YOU KIDDING? WHERE IS HE?
YOU CAN'T ACTUALLY WANT TO DO THIS NOW.
I'VE BEEN WAITING IN SOMEONE ELSE'S HEAD FOR FIVE YEARS. OF COURSE I WANT TO DO IT NOW. YOU GOT ONE OF THE BODIES, RIGHT?
WE GOT ONE OF THE ORIGINAL BODIES, YES.

PERFECT. SO WE USE THE BODY TO HACK INTO DANIEL AND TAKE IT OVER USING THE ENTRY CODE NUMBERS RAVEN HAS. SO SIMPLE IT'S ALMOST LIKE WE PLANNED IT THAT WAY.
LET'S GO GET THEM.

WHAT AM I TO DO, THEN?

THEY'VE GOT SCOUT DRONES CAMPED OUT ON ALL SIDES RIGHT NOW. I NEED ONE OF THEIR HEADS.

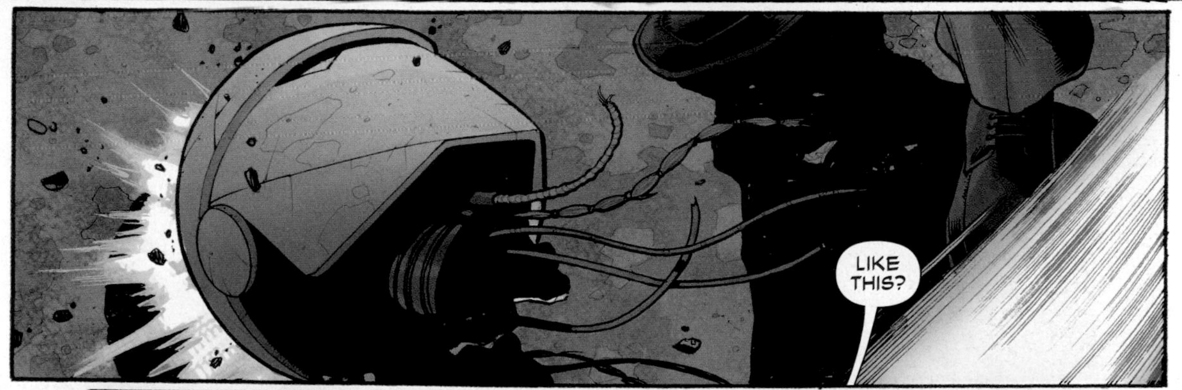
LIKE THIS?

YEAH, JUST LIKE THAT.
WHAT WILL IT DO?
BILLIONS OF DOLLARS AND THE MOST IMPRESSIVE TERRORIST NETWORK IN THE WORLD, THEY STILL PUT EVERYTHING ON THE SAME SERVER.
IT'S EMBARRASSING HOW MANY WARS GET WON AND LOST ON ENTRY LEVEL I.T.

Professor Dunn.
Wake up.
WHY DID YOU NOT DO THIS BEFORE?
IT'S GOOD FOR ALL OF TEN SECONDS. SECURITY SYSTEM'S ALREADY LOCKING ME OUT NOW. COME ON--
"--THINGS GET DECIDEDLY MORE OLD-SCHOOL FROM HERE."

I'VE BEEN WAITING A LONG TIME TO MEET YOU, YOU KNOW.
THEY KEEP TELLING ME ABOUT ALL THESE THINGS THAT HAPPENED WHILE I WAS AWAY-- IT'S WEIRD. AND WHAT THEY KEEP MENTIONING--MORE THAN ANYTHING, REALLY--IS HOW HARD YOU'VE BEEN FIGHTING. HOW, NO MATTER WHAT, YOU WON'T GIVE THEM WHAT THEY WANT.
THE SAD THING IS--EVERYBODY HERE ADMIRES THAT. THEY DO. THAT'S WHY THEY SEEM SO ANGRY.
BUT I'M NOT. BECAUSE I GET TO WALK IN HERE AND BE THE SOLUTION. I SPENT YEARS HIDING OUT THERE SO I COULD GET THIS TO YOU. SO THAT YOU WON'T HAVE TO SUFFER ANYMORE, AND NEITHER WILL WE. AND MOST IMPORTANTLY, I GUESS, NEITHER WILL THE PEOPLE WE'RE FIGHTING FOR.
"YEAH, YEAH, GREAT--BUT, KID, ONE LAST REQUEST--"

--DO WHAT YOU GOTTA DO, BUT SPARE ME THE PART WHERE YOU TALK GREATER GOOD. I'M AN OLD MAN, I HEARD ENOUGH OF THAT TO LAST ME WHATEVER I GOT LEFT.
JUST GET THIS OVER WITH.
FINE. FAIR ENOUGH. YOU REMEMBER THIS, DON'T YOU? THE MENTHOR HELMET. USES TELEPORTED QUANTUM D.N.A. IMPRINTS TO READ AND CONTROL THE BRAIN. VERY HELPFUL IN INTERROGATION-TYPE SITUATIONS.
THE GOOD NEWS IS, YOU CAN RELAX. YOU'RE NOT GOING TO HAVE TO BETRAY ANYONE.
JAMES, WE'RE GETTING SOME NOISE UPSTAIRS. WE NEED TO HURRY--
WOW, EVERYONE'S ALWAYS IN A RUSH. NO APPRECIATION FOR DIALOGUE. OKAY, LET'S GET GOING THEN, YEAH?

WHAT ARE THE--
...
WHAT ARE THE--
JAMES, ARE YOU OKAY?
HEY, LITTLE GUY, YOU FEELING ALL--

BLAM
BLA
THOOM
BLAM
DRONES! BACKUP, NOW!

JESUS CHRIST--
FRASER!
BLAM
BLAM
KRSSH

TOBY?
HELL... ARE YOU ALL RIGHT?
COLLEEN, HEY...

WHAT HAPPENED?!?
LISTEN... I-- I'M REALLY SORRY. I DIDN'T WANNA HURT ANYONE... SERIOUSLY... I TOLD HIM I DIDN'T WANNA HURT ANYONE...
DAMN IT.

JUST RELAX-- I'M GETTING YOU OUT OF HERE.
WAIT... HOLD ON... WHERE'S MY BROTHER?
...WHERE'S MY BROTHER?

Cover by **John Cassaday** & **Alex Sinclair**, after **Wally Wood**

COLLEEN?
SHUT UP AND LISTEN--WE GET BACK THERE, YOU DON'T SAY A WORD UNTIL I TELL YOU TO--
--GOT IT?
YEAH, BUT-- COLLEEN, HEY...

SCARED LITTLE GIRLS

NICK SPENCER: WRITER CAFU: PENCILLER
BIT: INKER SANTIAGO ARCAS: COLORIST PATRICK BROSSEAU: LETTERER

DON'T WORRY ABOUT THAT NOW. TOBY, PLEASE, PAY ATTENTION-- WHEN WE'RE BACK, JUST KEEP QUIET AND FOLLOW MY LEAD. DO YOU UNDERSTAND?
SURE... SURE...

MORNING.

YOU REMEMBER WHAT I TOLD YOU ON THE CHOPPER?
UHNN... YEAH.

IN TEN SECONDS, KEANE IS GOING TO COME IN HERE WITH A BIG SMILE ON HIS FACE. ***DON'T TALK.***

THERE HE IS. HOW YOU FEELING, SON?

STUPID QUESTION, I'VE BEEN HIT A FEW TIMES MYSELF. LISTEN, I ONLY HAVE A MINUTE, BUT I WANTED TO STOP BY AND SAY THANK YOU.
"THANK YOU"?

COLLEEN SAID YOU PERFORMED ADMIRABLY OUT THERE. I KNOW THAT CAN'T HAVE BEEN AN EASY THING TO DO. IT'S AN HONOR TO WELCOME YOU ABOARD, TOBY--
"ABOARD"?

BEEN A LONG TIME SINCE WE HAD A MENTHOR ON THE TEAM.

WELL, I'LL LEAVE YOU ALONE FOR NOW. COLLEEN, MY OFFICE IN TWENTY?

OKAY, WHAT JUST HAPPENED THERE?
THEY THINK YOU HAVING THE HELMET WAS PART OF THE PLAN. SO AS OF NOW, *IT WAS.*
DO--DO YOU KNOW WHO I REALLY AM?
I KNOW WHO YOU *WERE,* YES.

THEN WHY ARE YOU DOING THIS?

YOU NEED TO GET SOME REST.
WAIT-- THE AGENTS... DID THEY--
DID EVERYBODY MAKE IT BACK?

"YOU'VE ALREADY LIVED LONGER THAN ANY OF US EVER COULD.
"IF YOU'RE REALLY STARTING TO LOSE WHAT MADE YOU *YOU* IN THE FIRST PLACE--

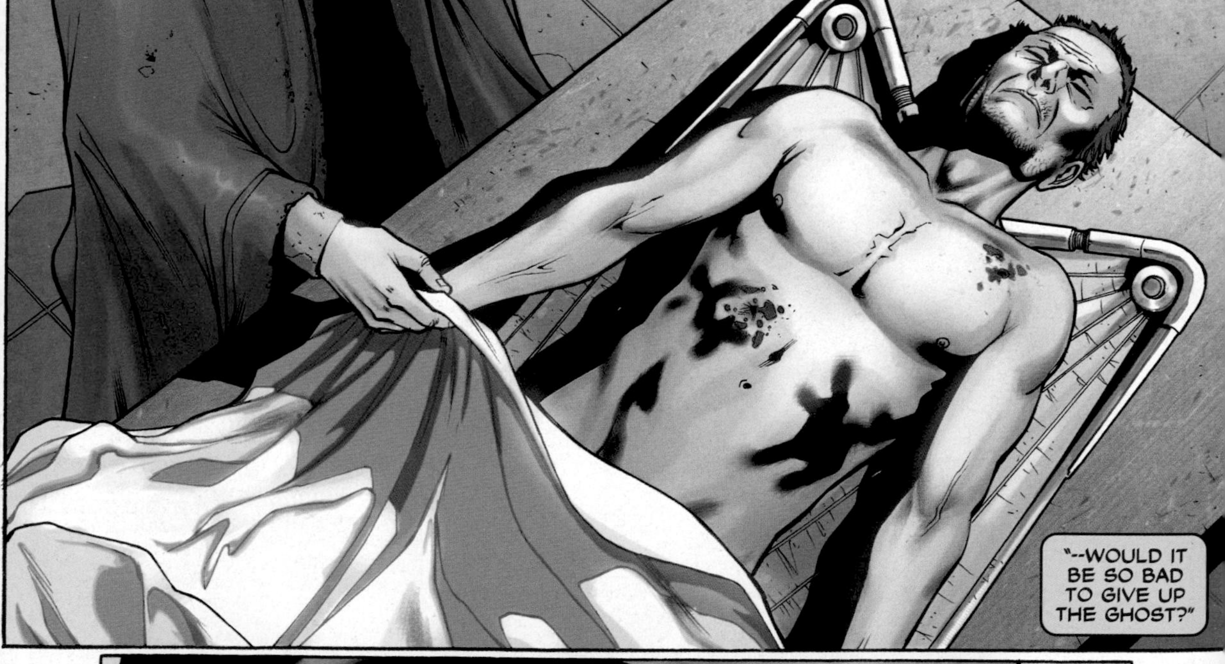
"--WOULD IT BE SO BAD TO GIVE UP THE GHOST?"

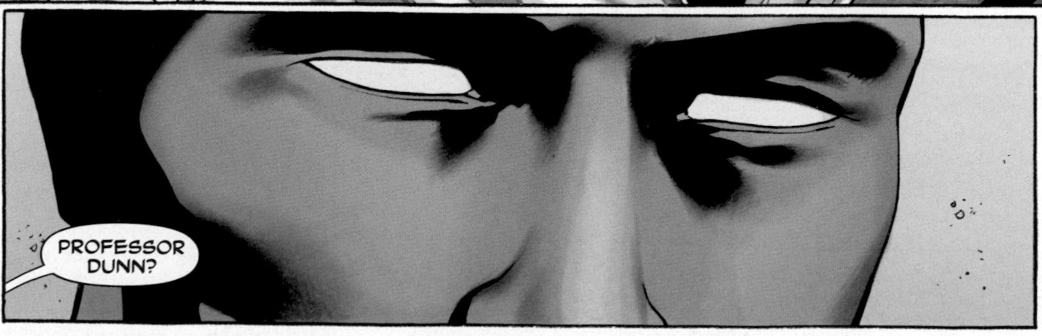
PROFESSOR DUNN?

I--I'M SORRY, SIR--
HM?
I--I'M TOLD TIME IS OF THE ESSENCE.
WE HAVE TO REMOVE THE WINGS RIGHT AWAY, SIR.
MM. YES--
YES, OF COURSE.

ERIC?
THE DOCTOR WILL SEE YOU NOW.
HAVE A SEAT, PLEASE--
HEY DOC, THANKS FOR FITTIN' ME IN. LISTEN, I NEED TO TELL YOU SOMETHIN'--

SINCE I TURNED THAT BELT ON BACK THERE, I BEEN GETTING THESE SHAKES--
THAT'S NORMAL, I'M AFRAID.

YEAH, BUT THESE THINGS-- IT FEELS LIKE THERE'S A TRAIN RUNNIN' THROUGH ME...LIKE I'M 'BOUT TO BREAK APART. AND IT JUST KEEPS COMIN', EVERY TIME I SIT STILL.
THAT'S NORMAL. TAKE YOUR SHIRT OFF FOR ME, PLEASE.

AND MY HEAD... MY DAMN HEAD'S JUST BEEN POUNDIN'--

THAT'S NORMAL. **DEEP BREATH.**

NEVER BE IN A HURRY. YOU'LL MISS THE BEST PARTS OF LIFE.
YOU DON'T UNDERSTAND--
RING! RING!

RING! RING!

HELLO?

HELLO?

AMELIA, WHO IS IT?
THEY'RE NOT SAYING ANYTHING!
THEN HANG UP!
HELLO?
HELLO?

ALL THAT DYING JUST SO SOMEONE COULD ASK A QUESTION.
I DON'T WANT TO HEAR YOU BEATING YOURSELF UP OVER THE COLLATERAL. WE'LL WORK WITH THE SRI LANKANS TO MAKE IT RIGHT.
"MAKE IT RIGHT"?
YOU DID THE BEST YOU COULD, NO ONE HOLDS YOU RESPONSIBLE FOR THAT.
BUT, I DO HAVE TO TELL YOU-- RECRUITING A NEW MENTHOR IN SECRET, STEALING THE HELMET--THAT'S NOT GOING TO BE EASY FOR ME TO EXPLAIN TO MY SUPERIORS.
WE WERE TOO COMPROMISED. I NEEDED TO KEEP SOMETHING OFF THE TABLE.
YOU COULD HAVE AT LEAST TOLD ME, THOUGH.
HOW DO I KNOW YOU'RE NOT SPIDER?
GOOD GIRL.

WHY HENSTON, THOUGH? I'D NEVER'VE GUESSED THE KID HAD IT IN HIM.
TOBY? I THINK YOU'D BE SURPRISED.
WELL, HE'S GOT NERVE, AT LEAST. TOUGH ORDER--BUT IF RAVEN COULDN'T BE EXTRACTED, WE HAD TO TERMINATE. IT WAS A DAMN SHAME, BUT THAT INFORMATION WAS TOO IMPORTANT TO GET LOOSE.

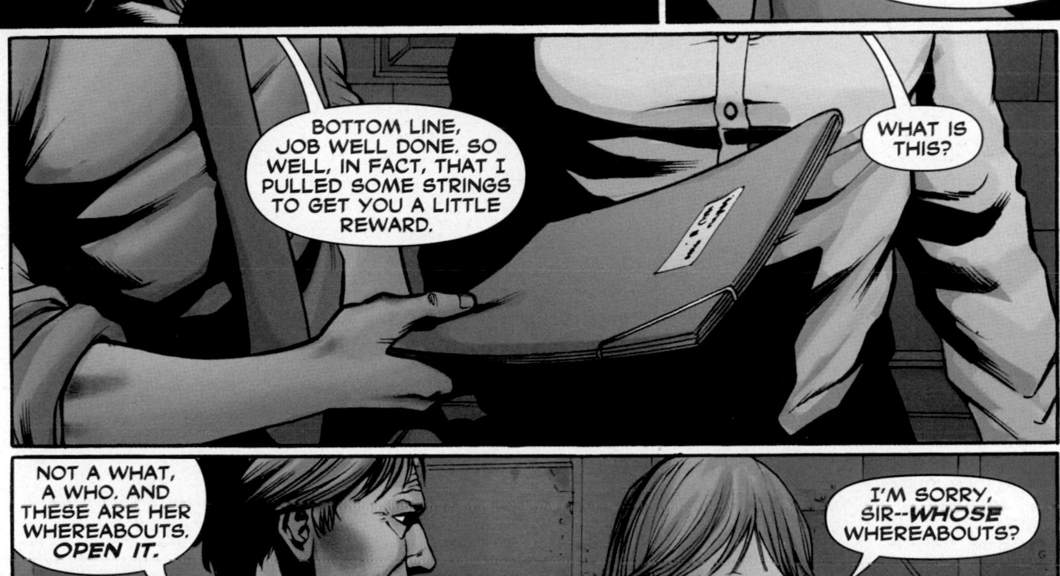
BOTTOM LINE, JOB WELL DONE. SO WELL, IN FACT, THAT I PULLED SOME STRINGS TO GET YOU A LITTLE REWARD.
WHAT IS THIS?

NOT A WHAT, A WHO. AND THESE ARE HER WHEREABOUTS. ***OPEN IT.***
I'M SORRY, SIR--***WHOSE*** WHEREABOUTS?

YOUR MOTHER'S.

THEY TOOK AMAL TAHA WHEN SHE WAS NINE.
THE SHEIKH LIKED HIS BRIDES YOUNG, AND HELPLESS.
HE WAS A MAN WHO ENJOYED SUFFERING.
THE OTHER GIRLS--SHE CALLED THEM HER SISTERS--SOME OF THEM HAD BEEN THERE FOR YEARS.
THEY TOLD STORIES OF WHAT HAPPENED TO THOSE WHO TRIED TO RUN AWAY. TERRIBLE STORIES OF TORTURE AND MUTILATION.
ONCE, SOME OF THEM TRIED TO HANG THEMSELVES. WHEN THE GUARDS CAUGHT THEM, THEY WERE BEATEN FOR HOURS, THEIR SCREAMS RINGING ALL THROUGH THE VILLA.
IN THE MORNINGS, WHILE THEIR TORMENTOR SLEPT, THEY HUDDLED TOGETHER, PRAYING TO GOD FOR RESCUE--OR, SPARING THAT, DEATH.
BUT AS TIME CREPT BY, MOST OF THEM SIMPLY ABANDONED ANY OF THE HOPES THEY ONCE CLUNG TO.

UNTIL THE DAY *SHE* CAME.
WITH GUNS AND FIRE BEHIND HER.
THE IRON MAIDEN.

SHEIKH FAROUK AMMAS--YOU'VE BEEN A BAD ENOUGH MAN TO MAKE YOURSELF *VERY* PROFITABLE TO KILL.
PLEASE-- NO--
AH, DON'T WORRY--
--I'M NOT GOING TO LAY A HAND ON YOU.
AMAL CAN SENSE THE TERROR IN HER SISTERS' HEARTS. EVEN NOW, EVEN AS HE SITS BROKEN BEFORE THEM, THEY FEAR HIM. THEY COWER, THEY CRY, AND STILL THEY PRAY FOR HELP.

AND IN THAT MOMENT, SHE REALIZES SHE IS NOT LIKE HER SISTERS.

SHE FEELS NO FEAR. SHE WHISPERS NO PRAYERS. ALL SHE NEEDS--

--IS RIGHT IN FRONT OF HER.

WHAT NOW, MADAME?
PUT HIS HEAD IN A BAG. KILL WHAT'S LEFT OF THE CREW, AND SCOUR THE SHIP FOR PARTS AND VALUABLES. THEN BURN IT DOWN TO THE WATER.
WHAT ABOUT THE CHILDREN?

TAKE HER.

LEAVE THE REST.

Cover by **Fiona Staples**

-belt longer
-gunbelt

NOW.
MORE WATER, MA'AM?
MM. THANK YOU.

MELBOURNE, AUSTRALIA.
TWENTY-EIGHT YEARS AGO.
OH, WELL, I'M THE TYPE OF GUY WHO WILL NEVER SETTLE DOWN--WHERE PRETTY GIRLS ARE, WELL, YOU KNOW THAT I'M AROUND--

I KISS 'EM AND I LOVE 'EM 'CAUSE TO ME THEY'RE ALL THE SAME--I HUG 'EM AND I SQUEEZE 'EM, THEY DON'T EVEN KNOW MY NAME--

THEY CALL ME THE WANDERER-- YEAH, THE WANDERER--

I ROAM AROUND, AROUND, AROUND--

OH, WELL, THERE'S FLO ON MY LEFT AND THERE'S MARY ON MY RIGHT--
AND JANIE IS THE GIRL THAT I'LL BE WITH TONIGHT--AND WHEN SHE ASKS ME WHICH ONE I LOVE THE BEST?
I TEAR OPEN MY SHIRT, I GOT ROSIE ON MY CHEST--

'CAUSE I'M THE WANDERER--YEAH, THE WANDERER--I ROAM AROUND, AROUND, AROUND--

OH, WELL, I ROAM FROM TOWN TO TOWN--I GO THROUGH LIFE WITHOUT A CARE--AND I'M AS HAPPY AS A CLOWN--
VEGEMI
Moo
Moo
Moo
Butter
Butter
Butter
Butter

I WITH MY TWO FISTS OF IRON AND I'M GOING NOWHERE--
Butter

RRINGG

HEY.

THE BANANA STRAWBERRY. COME ON, YOU KNOW THAT.
NO. NO-- SHE HATES THE APPLESAUCE.
THEN GO TO THE PLACE ON VICTORIA. RIGHT. NEXT TO THE FLORIST. THEY'LL HAVE IT.
OF COURSE I KNOW IT'S MORE EXPENSIVE, THAT'S WHY I DIDN'T SEND YOU THERE IN THE FIRST PLACE. HOLD ON--

HUUURK!!!

--SOMEONE'S AT THE DOOR.

WELL, AREN'T YOU A SIGHT FOR SORE EYES.

YOU BRING ANY MORE FRIENDS TO PLAY WITH, LITTLE BOY?

RIGHT--

--OF COURSE YOU DID.

ON VICTORIA
NICK SPENCER: WRITER
CAFU: PENCILLER BIT: INKER SANTIAGO ARCAS: COLORIST [PRESENT DAY SEQUENCE]
MIKE GRELL: ARTIST VAL STAPLES: COLORIST ['80s SEQUENCE]
NICK DRAGOTTA: ARTIST LEE LOUGHRIDGE: COLORIST ['60s SEQUENCE]
PATRICK BROSSEAU: LETTERER

--SOMEONE'S AT THE DOOR.
THERE HE IS!

STOP!
DON'T DO THIS, BROWN!

UNH!

LEN BROWN, FORMERLY KNOWN AS THE T.H.U.N.D.E.R. AGENT CODENAMED *DYNAMO*--

--YOU ARE HEREBY PLACED UNDER ARREST BY AUTHORITY OF THE HIGHER UNITED NATIONS WAR CRIMES TRIBUNAL--

--FOR AIDING AND HARBORING THE FUGITIVE KNOWN AS *THE IRON MAIDEN.*

JESUS--

YEAH. TWO MORE COMING OUT...
DOA

THAT'S HER. I'LL BE DAMNED. THAT'S HER.

WATCH YOUR HEAD, LEN.

SIR?
WHAT SHOULD WE DO ABOUT THIS ONE?

NOW.
MISS FRANKLIN? WELCOME TO MOROCCO.
COLLEEN FRANKLIN
SO WHAT BRINGS YOU HERE?
AH, YOU KNOW, THE USUAL--SEE THE SIGHTS, RELAX A BIT...
KILL MY MOTHER.

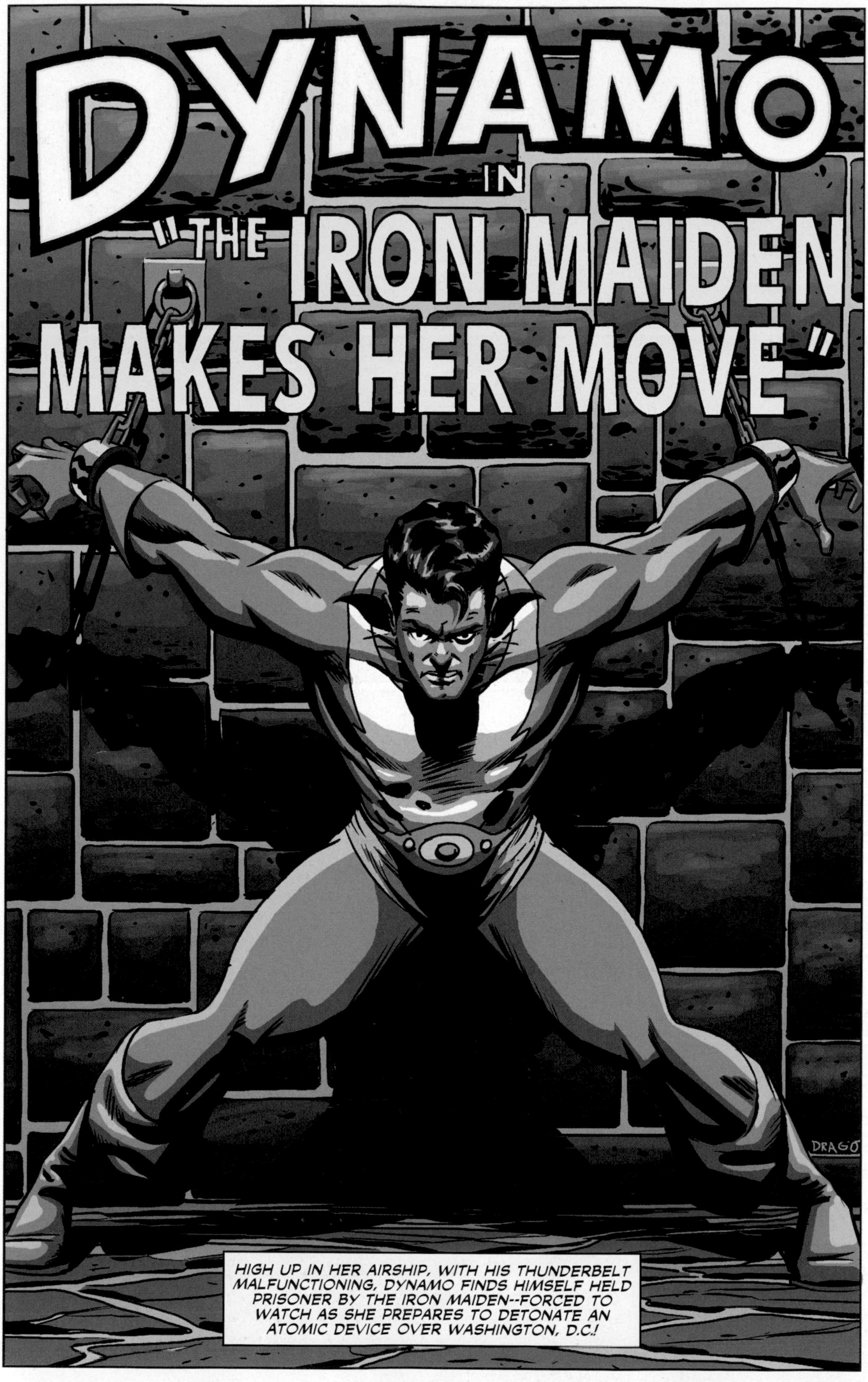

DYNAMO

IN

"THE IRON MAIDEN MAKES HER MOVE"

HIGH UP IN HER AIRSHIP, WITH HIS THUNDERBELT MALFUNCTIONING, DYNAMO FINDS HIMSELF HELD PRISONER BY THE IRON MAIDEN--FORCED TO WATCH AS SHE PREPARES TO DETONATE AN ATOMIC DEVICE OVER WASHINGTON, D.C.!

DRAGO

INSIDE THE MILITARY BASE ONCE SEIZED BY THE IRON MAIDEN, LIGHTNING AND THE T.H.U.N.D.E.R. SQUAD RACE TO GET CONTROL OF THE "WORLD KILLER" BOMB BEFORE IT'S DROPPED ON THE CAPITAL...
BETTER HURRY, KITTY! IF THAT BOMB GOES OFF, WE'RE ALL DONE FOR!
JUST NEED A SECOND MORE...

BEEP BEEP BEEP
THERE! I'VE CHANGED THE RADIO DETONATOR'S SIGNAL, SO THE BOMB'S COUNTDOWN HAS ALREADY STARTED!

WHICH MEANS THE ONLY ONES GETTIN' BLOWN TO HEAVEN TODAY ARE THE IRON MAIDEN AND HER LACKEYS ON THAT AIRSHIP!
BUT WHAT ABOUT DYNAMO?! SHE'S GOT HIM--HE'LL BE KILLED UP THERE, TOO!
HE'D UNDERSTAND WE CAN'T LET THAT BOMB GO OFF AND KILL ALL THOSE INNOCENT PEOPLE! BESIDES, I WOULDN'T GIVE UP ON HIM JUST YET, ANYWAY!
IT'S TRUE! DYNAMO'S BEEN IN A JAM BEFORE AND GOTTEN OUT JUST FINE! YOU GOTTA HAVE FAITH!

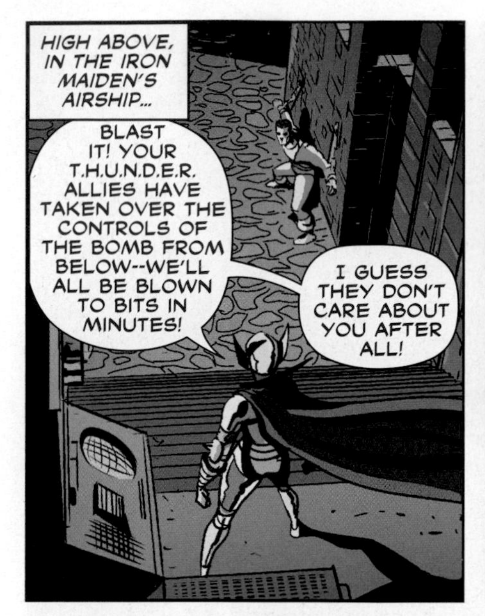
HIGH ABOVE, IN THE IRON MAIDEN'S AIRSHIP...
BLAST IT! YOUR T.H.U.N.D.E.R. ALLIES HAVE TAKEN OVER THE CONTROLS OF THE BOMB FROM BELOW--WE'LL ALL BE BLOWN TO BITS IN MINUTES!
I GUESS THEY DON'T CARE ABOUT YOU AFTER ALL!

THEY JUST KNOW I'D RATHER DIE THAN LET YOU ACTIVATE THAT BOMB OVER WASHINGTON! I TOLD YOU, YOU'LL NEVER BEAT US, IRON MAIDEN--I DON'T KNOW WHY YOU BOTHER TO TRY!
MAYBE I JUST ENJOY THE COMPANY OF A MAN LIKE YOURSELF, DYNAMO! NOW WHAT DO YOU THINK OF THAT?

I'D SAY THERE ARE BETTER WAYS TO GO ABOUT GETTING MY ATTENTION!
OR MAYBE YOU COULD JUST JOIN OUR SIDE INSTEAD!

SORRY--NOT MY STYLE, BEAUTIFUL!
THEN I GUESS YOU LEAVE ME NO CHOICE...
GO ON THEN! DO WHAT YOU WILL!

SHOULDN'T DO THIS, BUT--EVER SINCE WE MET, I'VE LOVED HER! AND WHY NOT? I DESERVE SOME HAPPINESS IN MY LIFE!
THIS MIGHT BE THE LAST CHANCE I GET TO SHOW HIM HOW I FEEL!

I'VE WAITED SO LONG TO DO THAT...
I HAVE TO SAY, IT DID FEEL RIGHT! TOO BAD IT MIGHT BE THE LAST THING WE EVER DO!

NO! I WON'T LET THAT HAPPEN. THERE'S THE EMERGENCY HATCH--IF WE DROP YOU OUT OF IT, I'M SURE YOUR FRIEND RAVEN CAN CATCH YOU!

BUT WHAT ABOUT YOU? YOU'LL DIE WHEN THE BOMB GOES OFF!
I'LL BE FINE--I HAVE AN ESCAPE POD! BUT IT ONLY FITS ONE, AND WILL TAKE ME DIRECTLY BACK TO MY EMPLOYERS!

YOU MUST NEVER TELL ANYONE WHAT HAPPENED BETWEEN US HERE--IT MUST REMAIN OUR SECRET!
ER, DON'T WORRY, LADY--I WON'T!

NOW GO! AND DON'T SAY I NEVER DID YOU ANY FAVORS!

DOWN BELOW, ON THE GROUND...
LOOK! UP THERE! DYNAMO'S BEEN TOSSED OUT OF THE AIRSHIP--WITH THE THUNDERBELT NOT WORKING, HE WON'T SURVIVE THAT FALL!

I THINK I CAN BE OF SOME ASSISTANCE HERE!

NOT GOING TO BE AN EASY CATCH, BUT--

--I'VE GOT YOU!

AT THAT EXACT MOMENT...
BA-ROOM

AND JUST IN TIME, TOO, IT LOOKS LIKE!
YOU GOT THAT RIGHT!

THE IRON MAIDEN'S SHIP, IT'S GONE UP IN FLAMES--GOOD RIDDANCE! LOOKS LIKE YOU WON'T HAVE TO WORRY ABOUT HER CHAINING YOU UP ANYMORE, DYNAMO!
ER, SURE--GOOD THING!

Cover by **Fiona Staples**

MOROCCO.
NOW.

1668
KNOCK KNOCK
ONE SECOND...

WHO ARE YOU?
MY NAME IS COLLEEN FRANKLIN. I'M WITH THE HIGHER UNITED NATIONS.

SIGH
FINALLY.

I WAS BEGINNING TO THINK YOU WEREN'T GOING TO SHOW.
1668

IT'S ALL IN THERE, I WASN'T BLUFFING.
I'LL JUST CHECK FOR MYSELF.
ACCESS CODES, SECURITY PROTOCOLS, BACKGROUND ON HER TOP LIEUTENANTS--EVERYTHING YOU EVER WANTED WHEN IT COMES TO KILLING THE IRON MAIDEN, I GOT IT.
HOW LONG WERE YOU WITH HER?

EIGHT YEARS. SHE PICKED ME UP WHEN I WAS FIFTEEN--
--AFTER SHE RAIDED A PROSTITUTION RING IN MOSCOW. NOT THE NICEST GUYS.

ANYHOW, ONCE THE DEAL GOES THROUGH, IT'S ALL YOURS TO SAVE THE WORLD WITH--OR WHATEVER IT IS YOU PEOPLE DO. SO LONG AS WHEN THE OLD CRONE'S DEAD, I GET THE BANK ACCOUNT.

OF COURSE. THAT WAS THE DEAL.

FWIISH!
COLD-BLOODED OLD TIMES
NICK SPENCER: WRITER
DAN PANOSIAN: ARTIST BRAD ANDERSON: COLORIST [PRESENT DAY SEQUENCE]
MIKE GRELL: ARTIST VAL STAPLES: COLORIST ['80s SEQUENCE]
NICK DRAGOTTA: ARTIST LEE LOUGHRIDGE: COLORIST ['60s SEQUENCE]
PATRICK BROSSEAU: LETTERER

JUST LIKE
SORRY, WHAT'S THAT?
YOU...
YOU LOOK JUST LIKE HER.
FWIISH!

T.H.U.N.D.E.R. TOWER.
TWENTY-EIGHT YEARS AGO.
ONE MORE TIME, THEN:
NO CONTACT EXTREME DANGER STAY BEHIND RED LINE!
CHRISTOPHER JARRETT? ANY BELLS?
NO? OKAY, FINE, HOW ABOUT THIS ONE:
PAIGE JARRETT. CHRISTOPHER JARRETT'S FOUR-YEAR-OLD DAUGHTER.
YOU PROBABLY DON'T RECOGNIZE HER, THOUGH, WHAT WITH THE THIRD DEGREE BURNS AND ALL, BUT TRUST ME, SHE WAS DEFINITELY IN THEIR HOUSE THE DAY YOU BLEW IT UP.
WHICH REMINDS ME--

--YOU HAVE A DAUGHTER, TOO, DON'T YOU?

MAYBE THESE TWO COULD PLAY TOGETHER SOMETIME. I MEAN, IF YOUR KID CAN KEEP FROM SCREAMING OR THROWING UP WHEN SHE SEES PAIGE'S FACE. IT AIN'T PRETTY, YOU KNOW?

BUT DON'T GET ME WRONG HERE--IT'S NOT LIKE WE'RE NOT ALL FANS.

IN FACT, WE'RE CHECKING WITH GUINNESS ON THIS, BUT WE THINK YOU MIGHT'VE MADE HISTORY.
WE ARE FAIRLY CERTAIN THAT YOU--THE IRON MAIDEN--HAVE KILLED MORE PEOPLE THAN ANY ONE INDIVIDUAL WHO EVER WALKED GOD'S GREEN EARTH.

NOW SURE, HITLER, POL POT, STALIN--THEY GOT A HIGHER DEATH COUNT TECHNICALLY, BUT THEY DID IT GIVING ORDERS. I'M TALKING THE "WITH YOUR OWN TWO HANDS" BIT. THE FACE-TO-FACE.
YOU GET DOWN TO THAT, THEY CAN'T HOLD A CANDLE TO YOU. I MEAN, COME ON--
--FOUR THOUSAND, EIGHT HUNDRED AND NINETEEN.
FOUR THOUSAND, EIGHT HUNDRED AND NINETEEN.
THAT IS-- LYDIA, WHAT WOULD YOU CALL THAT?
INCREDIBLE, SIR.
DANGER
DAMN RIGHT. INCREDIBLE.
SO, LOOK, I GET IT, ALL THOSE PEOPLE, IT MUST BE REAL TOUGH REMEMBERING THEM ALL. I'M BAD WITH FACES MYSELF, BUT--
--NOTHING?
THAT'S FINE, NO PROBLEM. WE GOT TIME.

NOW.

CRAK
CRAK
CRAK

TWENTY-EIGHT YEARS AGO.
BILL!
LEN--
PLEASE,
SIT
DOWN.

I'M SO
GLAD YOU
CAME--
OKAY...
OKAY.
LET'S JUST
TRY TO--
--AW,
CHRIST,
LEN--

--HOW
COULD YOU
BE SO DAMN
STUPID?

I LOVE HER, BILL.
YOU--?SHE'S A TERRORIST!
SHE'S CHANGED.
SHE KILLED FOUR OF OUR MEN YESTERDAY WHEN THEY CAME TO GET HER!
THAT'S-- THAT'S DIFFERENT, AND YOU KNOW IT. SHE WAS ATTACKED, COLLEEN WAS IN--
DO YOU UNDERSTAND THE INTERNATIONAL INCIDENT YOU'VE TOUCHED OFF HERE?
TEN YEARS AGO, THE MOST DECORATED T.H.U.N.D.E.R. AGENT IN THE HISTORY OF THE PROGRAM RETIRES, THEN COMPLETELY FALLS OFF THE GRID--
--ONLY TO TURN UP NOW, HARBORING THE MOST SOUGHT-AFTER FUGITIVE ON THE PLANET, A WOMAN WE FOUGHT AGAINST FOR YEARS. YOU'RE SHACKED UP WITH THE @&$%&%$ IRON MAIDEN! YOU HAVE A KID WITH HER!
DO YOU REALIZE WHAT THAT WOULD DO TO THE AGENT PROJECT? TO THE HIGHER U.N.?
I DON'T GIVE A DAMN ABOUT THE HIGHER U.N.! SHE'S MY WIFE!
LEN-- LISTEN TO ME--KEEP YOUR VOICE DOWN!
WE NEVER WOULD'VE WON THE WAR WITHOUT HER.
A WAR NO ONE IS EVEN SUPPOSED TO KNOW ABOUT. WATCH IT WITH THAT.

BUT THEY LET HER GET AWAY AFTERWARDS! WE THOUGHT THE COUNCIL WOULD...LOOK THE OTHER WAY AFTER WHAT WE'D DONE--WE SAVED THE WORLD, DAMN IT! DON'T YOU PEOPLE CARE ABOUT ANY--
LEN, THIS IS WHY YOU GET IMMUNITY DEALS ON PAPER. IF THERE WAS ANY KIND OF AGREEMENT, ANYTHING ON RECORD, MAYBE WE COULD--
NO...NO. NOTHING LIKE THAT.
THEN THAT'S NO HELP TO ME.
WHAT'S GOING TO HAPPEN?
DON'T WORRY. THIS--THIS IS TOO BIG TO GET OUT. WE'RE NOT SENDING DYNAMO TO PRISON. NO ONE WANTS ANYTHING PUBLIC. IT WOULD DESTROY EVERYTHING WE'VE BUILT HERE.
YOU AND THE BABY WILL BE FINE. THEY'LL SET YOU UP IN A SAFE HOUSE SOMEWHERE.
WHAT ABOUT RUSTY?
IT'S WAY TOO LATE FOR THAT.
NO.
SHE'S A BUTCHER, LEN. DO YOU HAVE ANY IDEA HOW MANY DIGNITARIES, HOW MANY HEADS OF STATE SHE'S KILLED? NO WAY WILL THEY LET HER--
NO!

I'M SORRY, LEN, THIS IS WAY OVER MY HEAD. TOO MANY PEOPLE WANT HER DEAD. AND QUITE FRANKLY, SHE DESERVES IT. I CAN'T HELP YOU--
BUT THERE *HAS* TO BE A WAY! I--THERE *HAS* TO BE SOMETHING YOU CAN DO--
--THERE HAS TO BE.
LOOK, LEN--THERE *MIGHT*--THERE MIGHT BE SOMETHING WE CAN WORK OUT, IF THAT'S REALLY WHAT YOU WANT--
--BUT, *AS YOUR FRIEND,* I'M TELLING YOU--
--YOU NEED TO THINK ABOUT THAT DAUGHTER OF YOURS.

NOW.
WAKE HER. NOW. HURRY.
YES, MA'AM.
DID YOU HEAR ME, DAMN IT?! I SAID, HU--
BLAM

MADAME-- I'M SO SORRY--WE HAVE AN INTRUDER AT THE GATE!
WHAT?
HENDRA AND SALA ARE BOTH DEAD--HALF OF THE CAMERAS ARE OUT--
QUIET, GIRL--LET'S HAVE A LOOK THEN...
DO YOU KNOW HER, MADAME?
OF COURSE I DO, DARLING--
--SHE'S MY DAUGHTER.

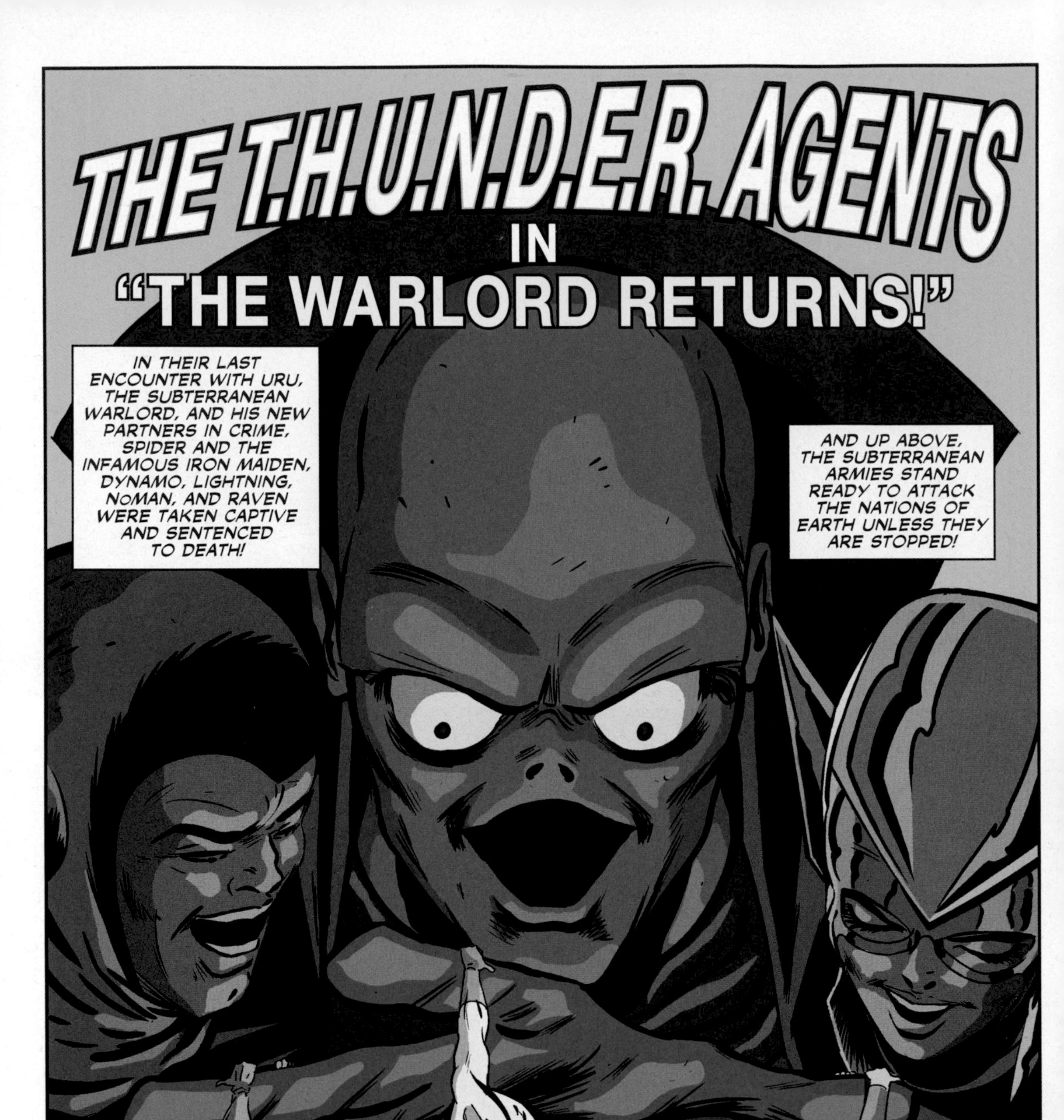
THE T.H.U.N.D.E.R. AGENTS
IN
"THE WARLORD RETURNS!"
IN THEIR LAST ENCOUNTER WITH URU, THE SUBTERRANEAN WARLORD, AND HIS NEW PARTNERS IN CRIME, SPIDER AND THE INFAMOUS IRON MAIDEN, DYNAMO, LIGHTNING, NoMAN, AND RAVEN WERE TAKEN CAPTIVE AND SENTENCED TO DEATH!
AND UP ABOVE, THE SUBTERRANEAN ARMIES STAND READY TO ATTACK THE NATIONS OF EARTH UNLESS THEY ARE STOPPED!

HA, LOOK AT YOU NOW, T.H.U.N.D.E.R. AGENTS! FOR MONTHS WE'VE BEEN FIGHTING IN THESE TUNNELS, BUT NOW MY ARMIES STAND READY TO INVADE THE SURFACE--
--STRONGER THAN EVER, AND UNITED WITH SPIDER AND THE IRON MAIDEN!

THOSE BONDS WE PUT YOU IN NEGATE YOUR POWERS. SO NOW WE'RE GOING TO WATCH ALL OF YOU DIE...SLOWLY!
BUT WAIT, YOU TOLD ME IF I JOINED YOU, YOU WOULD SPARE DYNAMO'S LIFE! YOU CAN'T DO THIS, I LOVE HIM!

FOOLISH WOMAN! I ONLY TOLD YOU THAT TO GET YOU ON OUR SIDE! I WOULD NEVER LET SOMEONE AS DANGEROUS AS DYNAMO LIVE!

I'M AFRAID OUR ARRANGEMENT IS OVER THEN, "BOSS"!
BOOM

SHE'S FREEING US! WAY TO GO, IRON MAIDEN!
LOOKS LIKE WE MAY HAVE BEEN WRONG ABOUT YOU!

NOW FREED FROM URU'S CHAINS, DYNAMO BEGINS THE BATTLE ANEW!
THOOM
JOINED BY LIGHTNING, WITH HIS SUPER-SPEED!
WAMBAM
KCHAK
NOMAN WORKS IN THE SHADOWS--
--AND RAVEN ATTACKS FROM ABOVE!
POP

NOW CALL YOUR MEN OFF! THIS WAR IS OVER BEFORE IT'S BEGUN!

ATTENTION, ALL SUBTERRANEAN SOLDIERS! RETURN TO BASE!

FOLLOWING THEIR LEADER'S ORDERS, THE SUBTERRANEANS TURN AND HEAD BACK TO THEIR UNDERGROUND HOMES...

WE CAN ALL FINALLY GO HOME, TEAM!

BACK ON THE T.H.U.N.D.E.R. JET...
GOOD WORK, AGENTS!

UNFORTUNATELY, THE WORLD MUST NEVER KNOW WHAT YOU DID HERE, OR ELSE THE POPULATION WOULD BE TERRIFIED OF THE DANGERS LIVING BELOW THE SURFACE!

BUT DON'T WORRY, WE'LL MAKE SURE YOU'RE ALL REWARDED FOR YOUR HARD WORK WHEN YOU RETURN!
THANK YOU, SIR! BUT WHAT ABOUT THE IRON MAIDEN? SHE TOOK OFF AFTER GETTING US OUT OF THAT JAM!

WE'LL LET HER GO. OBVIOUSLY SHE DID US A GREAT SERVICE RESCUING YOU MEN!
GREAT TO HEAR, DIRECTOR! I THINK THERE'S MORE TO THAT LADY THAN WE REALIZE!

Cover by Fiona Staples
FS'11

1

2

3

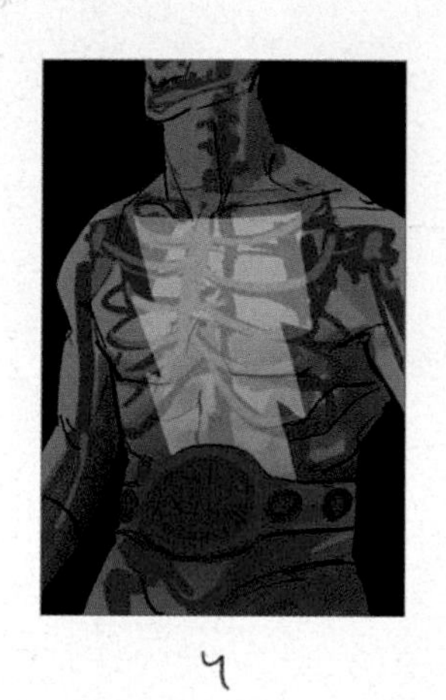

4

5

TWENTY-EIGHT YEARS AGO.
EXTREME
DANGER
STAY BEHIND
LINE!
YOURS ALWAYS
NICK SPENCER: WRITER
DAN PANOSIAN: ARTIST BRAD ANDERSON COLORIST (PRESENT DAY SEQUENCE)
MIKE GRELL: ARTIST VAL STAPLES: COLORIST ('80s SEQUENCE)
NICK DRAGOTTA: ARTIST LEE LOUGHRIDGE: COLORIST ('60s SEQUENCE)
PATRICK BROSSEAU: LETTERER
Dear Rusty,

Well, you were right.
This is all my fault. I was always so damn trusting. And sloppy. I thought they would leave us alone. I thought we could stop hiding. I was a fool.
Now you're locked up and somewhere I can't hold you. And our baby is God knows where.
I want to tell you how sorry I am for failing you...
But words like those come cheap, don't they?

They've offered me a deal, and I've taken it. And I can't hear you right now, so there's no use yelling at me, Red.
Turns out I am a pretty special individual (told ya so), and they haven't been able to find anyone else out there able to play Dynamo for them.
They say me doing this will help them figure out how to make the belt so other people can use it. And I have already prayed to ask forgiveness for that.
But I'm going to take care of something for them down in Panama, and in exchange, they're going to let you and Colleen alone.
Don't worry, I made sure to get it in writing this time.

Now, I know you have never thought I was the brightest man to walk the earth...
But I am not so stupid as to not know what this means.
I know how just looking at that belt made this old body ache, so I can guess what it'll do once I put it on.
But I won't let you two down. Not this time.
I'll do what they want, and you'll be free. You won't ever have to run again..

Bill Henry was always a friend to me at T.H.U.N.D.E.R. He is a good man. He'll take care of you and Colleen. I told him to find a place with good schools.
Please let her know how much her Daddy loved her.
And as for you, I just want you to know I have never regretted any of it. Not even for a second.
You and me were meant to be together, and that's that.
Take care, beautiful. I love you.
Yours always,
Len

NOW.

YOU FINISHED?

THAT'S MY GUN.
DON'T WORRY, I'LL GIVE IT BACK TO YOU WHEN I'M DONE WITH IT.

YOU'VE GOT YOUR FATHER FOR BRAINS, YOU KNOW THAT?

DO IT.
CLICK
CLICK
DIDN'T LOAD IT.
NOW.

SORRY, MOTHER--

--I DIDN'T COME ALONE.

DYNAMO
IN
HAVING JUST TRIUMPHED OVER THE FORCES OF EVIL IN THE GREAT SUBTERRANEAN WAR, LEN BROWN--THE T.H.U.N.D.E.R. AGENT DYNAMO--HAS ANNOUNCED HIS RETIREMENT FROM T.H.U.N.D.E.R., EFFECTIVE IMMEDIATELY!
IS THIS REALLY...?
"A FAREWELL TO OUR HERO"

I JUST CAN'T BELIEVE IT! DYNAMO NO MORE!
YOU'VE BEEN A GOOD FRIEND TO ME, BILL, BUT MY MIND IS MADE UP! I'M THROUGH!
I GUESS THERE'S NOTHING I CAN SAY THEN, BUT...

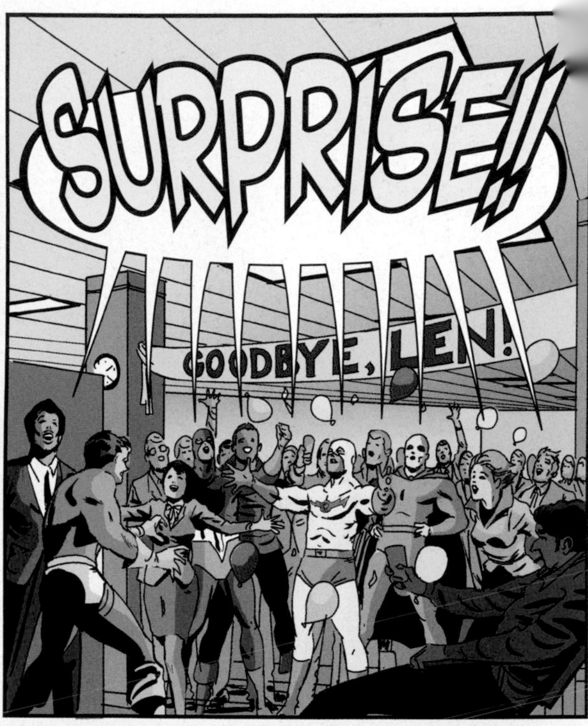
SURPRISE!!
GOODBYE, LEN!

WOW, GANG... I DON'T EVEN KNOW WHAT TO SAY! THIS IS TOO MUCH!
YOU DON'T HAVE TO SAY ANYTHING, LEN, YOU'VE ALREADY DONE ENOUGH!

KITTY! ALICE!
KITTY SAID IT! WE'RE ALL JUST REAL SORRY TO SEE YOU GO!

TH ALL THE AND WOMEN E'S SERVED ALONGSIDE GATHERED OGETHER, THE OUP BEGINS TO EMINISCE OVER ALL THE TIMES THEY'VE HAD...
THE ADVENTURES THEY SHARED...
THE DANGERS THEY FACED...
THE AMAZING THINGS THEY'VE SEEN....
AND THE THINGS THEY NEVER EXPECTED (AND MOST NEVER KNEW ABOUT).
AS THE TEARS AND BITTERSWEET ADIEUS SHOW NO SIGN OF STOPPING, LEN BROWN QUIETLY AND POLITELY EXCUSES HIMSELF...

...TO MAKE A QUICK TRIP TO VISIT THE GRAVE OF HIS FALLEN TEAMMATE AND FRIEND--MENTHOR!

I'VE TRIED TO HONOR YOUR MEMORY AS MUCH AS I CAN, JOHN...I KNOW YOU DIDN'T ALWAYS LIVE AS A HERO, BUT YOU SURE DIED AS ONE! I'D LIKE TO THINK YOU'D UNDERSTAND...
JOHN JANUS
"Greater love hath no man than that he lay down his life for his friend..."

I KNOW THE WORLD NEEDS A DYNAMO, BUT IT'S TIME FOR ME TO GO, I KNOW IT...IF I DON'T STOP NOW, I'M GOING TO END UP RIGHT THERE IN THE GROUND WITH YOU!

IF ONLY THE WORLD KNEW THE TERRIBLE PRICE WE PAY FOR THESE POWERS...

THAT EVENING, LEN BROWN MAKES HIS FINAL STOP AS DYNAMO...

...TO THE INNER COUNCIL OF T.H.U.N.D.E.R.!
THANK YOU AGAIN, BROWN, FOR YOUR YEARS OF SERVICE. I ONLY WISH YOU COULD STAY LONGER...
THIS MEANS, OF COURSE, WE'LL HAVE TO FIND SOMEONE NEW TO WEAR THE THUNDERBELT!

BUT A DEAL IS A DEAL, AND YOU DESERVE TO BE HONORED FOR YOUR SERVICE.
THANK YOU, SIR! I'VE DONE ALL I COULD!
WE ONLY HAVE ONE QUESTION AND THEN YOU'RE FREE TO GO: WHAT WILL YOU DO NEXT?

ER, YOU KNOW, IT'S STRANGE, BUT--I HADN'T REALLY THOUGHT ABOUT IT!

A GOOD QUESTION INDEED, ISN'T IT? WITH HIS DAYS OF SAVING THE WORLD BEHIND HIM, WHAT LIES NEXT FOR OUR HERO?
WE CAN'T ANSWER THAT JUST YET, DEAR READER, BUT NO MATTER WHAT, WE KNOW LEN BROWN IS STILL A HERO IN OUR HEARTS!

Cover by **Fiona Staples**

1

2

3

TWENTY-EIGHT YEARS AGO.
MORE WATER, MA'AM?
MM. THANK YOU.
SHE'LL LOVE IT.

THE NEIGHBORHOOD, I MEAN.
LOTS OF OTHER KIDS AROUND, A NICE PARK DOWN THE STREET...IT'S A GOOD PLACE TO GROW UP.
AND HOW MANY GUARDS WILL I HAVE?
SIGH LET'S JUST SAY IT'S A HEALTHY LINE ITEM IN SOMEONE'S BUDGET. YOU UNDERSTAND, RUSTY, THE DEAL LEN MADE, IT'S NOT AMNESTY--
--THIS IS COMPLETE AND TOTAL HOUSE ARREST. YOU'LL NEVER BE ALLOWED TO LEAVE THE PROPERTY. AS FAR AS YOUR NEIGHBORS ARE CONCERNED, YOU'RE SICK AND BEDRIDDEN, AND THOSE GUARDS ARE YOUR FULL-TIME CARE.
THIS AGREEMENT HAS BEEN CONSTRUCTED TO GIVE COLLEEN AS MUCH OF AN OPPORTUNITY TO LIVE A NORMAL LIFE AS POSSIBLE-- ONE THAT INCLUDES HER MOTHER. THAT WAS OUR PRIMARY FOCUS.
I SEE. TELL ME--BILL, IS IT?
BILL HENRY, YES. I SERVED WITH YOUR HUSBAND.
TELL ME, BILL, WHERE IS MY DAUGHTER NOW?

SHE'S, AH-- SHE'S STILL IN MELBOURNE, WITH A FOSTER FAMILY RIGHT NOW. WE THOUGHT IT WOULD BE BEST IF YOU GOT IN AND SETTLED BEFORE WE BROUGHT HER OVER. GIVEN THE SECURITY SITUATION AND ALL.
I SEE.
NOW, BEFORE WE LAND, WE DO NEED TO TALK ABOUT CHRISTOPHER JARRETT. I DIDN'T TELL--
IS THAT THE CAPTAIN?
AH, I'D ASSUME SO.
HM.
WHAT?
NO, IT'S JUST--IT'S FUNNY THE THINGS WE NEVER NOTICE.
FOR INSTANCE, YOU'RE THE ONLY MAN ON THIS FLIGHT.
THAT'S BY DESIGN, IN PART. LIKE I SAID BEFORE, YOUR GUARDS WILL BE POSING AS NURSES, AND STATISTICALLY SPEAKING--
OF COURSE. STATISTICALLY SPEAKING. JUST FUNNY.

YOU KNOW, I RECOGNIZE ONE OF THEM--SHE VISITED MY CELL WITH A RATHER OBNOXIOUS GENTLEMAN, NOT UNLIKE YOURSELF.
LYDIA, IS IT?
YES, MA'AM.

HM. AND--NOW THIS IS JUST A SHOT IN THE DARK, BUT--I'LL GO AHEAD AND SURMISE THAT THE PLAN TO HAVE ALL-FEMALE GUARDS POSING AS NURSES WAS ***HER*** PROPOSAL?
ER, YEAH, IT WAS IN FACT...

HM. AND--FORGIVE ME FOR THIS, BUT--LYDIA, WOULD I BE AT ALL OUT OF BOUNDS IN PRESUMING YOU'VE BEEN PAID A RATHER LARGE SUM OF MONEY FROM ASSOCIATES OF MINE, AND HAVE IN FACT PUT THIS TEAM TOGETHER IN ORDER TO EXTRACT ME?

THAT'S CORRECT, MA'AM.

NO--!
WONDERFUL. LYDIA, YOU CAN GO AHEAD AND KILL HIM NOW.

WAIT! RUSTY--THIS-- THIS ISN'T WHAT YOUR HUSBAND WOULD'VE WANTED!

MY HUSBAND IS DEAD.
YOU KILLED HIM.

ACCK--IF YOU DO THIS--YOU KNOW YOU'LL NEVER SEE YOUR DAUGHTER AGAIN...
YOU KNOW, ON SECOND THOUGHT--

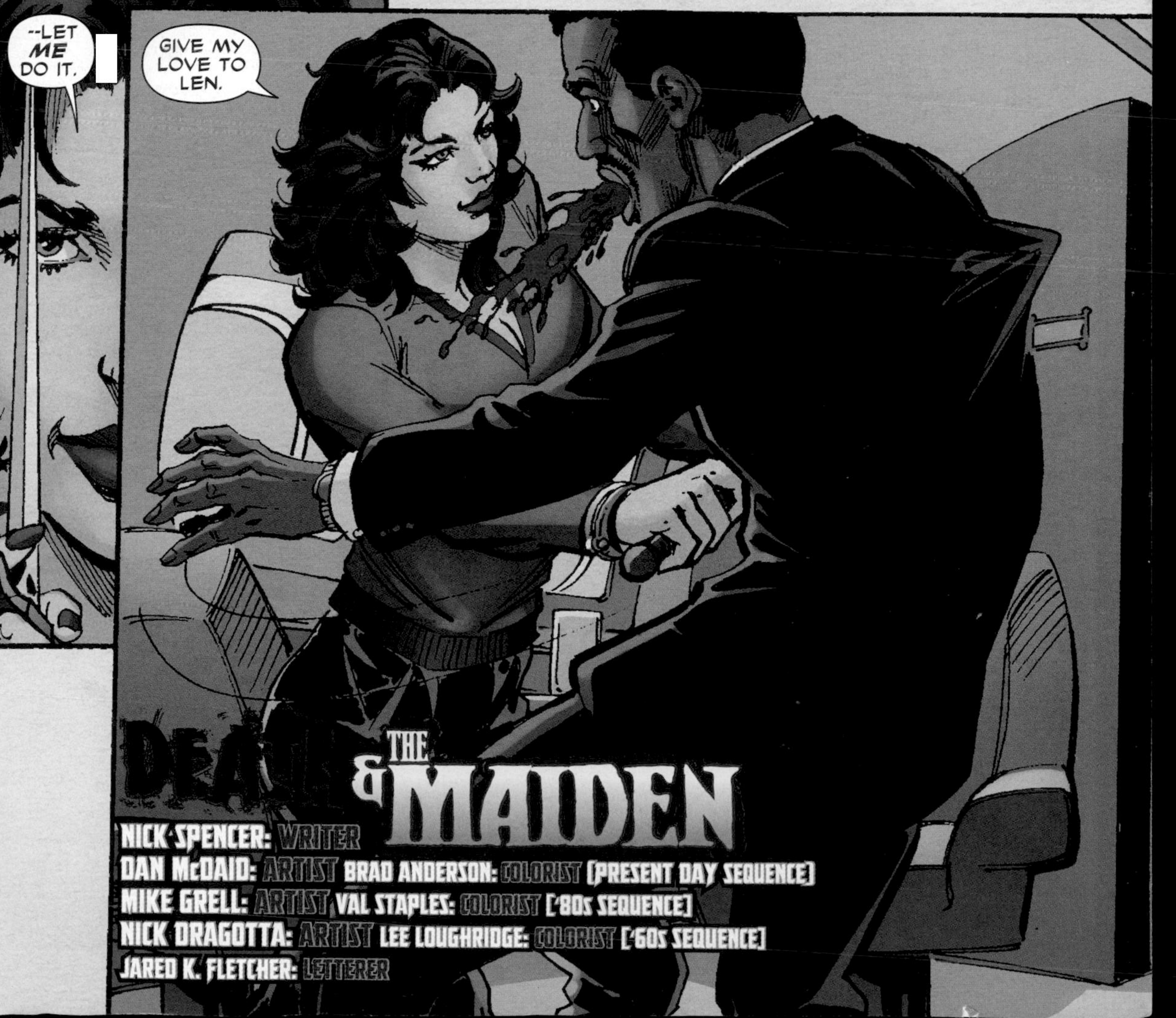
--LET ME DO IT.
GIVE MY LOVE TO LEN.
THE MAIDEN
NICK SPENCER: WRITER
DAN McDAID: ARTIST BRAD ANDERSON: COLORIST [PRESENT DAY SEQUENCE]
MIKE GRELL: ARTIST VAL STAPLES: COLORIST ['80s SEQUENCE]
NICK DRAGOTTA: ARTIST LEE LOUGHRIDGE: COLORIST ['60s SEQUENCE]
JARED K. FLETCHER: LETTERER

NOW.
LOOK AT YOU.

WORKING FOR THE MEN WHO KILLED YOUR OWN FATHER.

ALL WE WANTED WAS TO BE LEFT ALONE! WE SAVED THE WHOLE DAMN PLANET--WE ***DESERVED*** OUR HAPPINESS! THEY DID THIS!

YOU DISGUST ME.

CRACK
ALL OF YOU, OUTSIDE. THREE MINUTES.
TOBY-- EXCEPT YOU.
I NEED YOU TO PUT THE HELMET ON.
UMM... I FEEL OBLIGATED TO REMIND YOU HOW WELL IT WENT THE LAST TIME I DID THAT.
TOBY?
YEAH?
PUT THE DAMN HELMET ON.
OKAY, WELL--UM, IRON LADY, I APOLOGIZE IN ADVANCE IF I END UP SHOOTING YOU. THIS THING HAS SOME BUGS IN IT...
HURRY UP.

GOOD. NOW ASK FOR THE NUMBERS.
YOU LITTLE BITCH--I'LL RIP YOUR BLOODY--
NOW.
GIVE US THE NUMBERS.
GIVE US THE NUMBERS.

GOOD JOB, TOBY.
WHAT ARE YOU THANKING ME FOR?
YOU JUST GAVE HER EVERYTHING SHE EVER NEEDED, BOY. EVERYTHING HER SCHEMING, TRAITOROUS HEART EVER DESIRED.
CONGRATULATIONS ON OUTLIVING YOUR USEFULNESS.
BUT I SUPPOSE SHE'LL BE KILLING *ME* FIRST.
OH, *I'M* NOT GOING TO KILL YOU, MOTHER--

--SHE IS.
YOU REMEMBER PAIGE JARRETT, DON'T YOU? YOU MURDERED HER FATHER WHEN SHE WAS FOUR. LEFT HER WITH THIRD-DEGREE BURNS OVER MOST OF HER BODY.
WELL, SHE'S HAD A PRETTY BUSY LIFE SINCE THEN. SERVED IN THE ROYAL NAVY FOR A BIT, THEN WENT PRIVATE. SET UP HER OWN MERCENARY ARMY, VERY ACTIVE IN NORTH AFRICA RIGHT NOW.
SO WHEN WE FOUND YOU, I GAVE HER A CALL.
FOR WHICH I'M SURE SHE'LL BE ETERNALLY GRATEFUL.

I THOUGHT IT SHOULD BE HER THAT DOES IT, RATHER THAN ME.
BUT DO YOU KNOW WHY?

BECAUSE THE DAY YOU KILLED HER FATHER, I WAS THREE MONTHS OLD.

WHICH, OBVIOUSLY, SOMEWHAT CONTRADICTS THE WHOLE "WE JUST WANTED TO BE LEFT ALONE" BIT, YEAH?
ACCORDING TO YOU, THAT WAS LONG AFTER YOU'D RETIRED. LONG AFTER YOU'D TRADED IT ALL IN FOR THE DOMESTIC LIFE.

NOW, I COULD ASK WHY YOU RISKED EVERYTHING TO SNEAK AROUND AND DO A JOB WITHOUT YOUR HUSBAND EVEN KNOWING, AND WITH ME IN THE CRIB--
--BUT AFTER A LIFETIME OF READING EVERY FILE ON YOU, I SHOULD REALLY KNOW TO TRUST MY INSTINCTS ON YOUR BEHAVIOR BY NOW.

YOU WERE **BORED,** WEREN'T YOU?

GO ON, THEN. TELL ME I'M WRONG.
TELL ME IT WAS SOME KIND OF GRUDGE THAT YOU JUST COULDN'T LET GO OF. SOME KIND OF RIGHTEOUS VENGEANCE. THAT IT WASN'T JUST ANOTHER PAY-CHECK HIT.
TELL ME YOU WERE FORCED TO, THAT SOMEONE BLACK-MAILED YOU AND THEY WERE THREATENING TO KILL ME AND MY FATHER IF YOU DIDN'T DO IT.
TELL ME SOMETHING. TELL ME *ANYTHING.*
YOU ALWAYS DID CRY TOO MUCH, GIRL.
WE'RE DONE HERE.
COLLEEN--

--WAIT.
I CAN HELP YOU. I KNOW WHAT YOU'RE HIDING.
I KNOW HE'S STILL ALIVE.

COLLEEN, LISTEN TO ME--WE DON'T HAVE TO DO THIS. WE CAN BRING HER IN. YOU MADE YOUR POINT, IT'S NOT LIKE JARRETT CAN DO ANYTHING UNLESS WE LET--
TOBY, STOP.

LOOK, I'M JUST SAYING, SHE'S STILL, YOU KNOW...
WHAT?

SHE'S STILL YOUR ***MOTHER.***

ONLY FOR ABOUT ANOTHER THIRTY SECONDS.

BLAM

DYNAMO

IN

HAVING JUST RETIRED FROM T.H.U.N.D.E.R., **LEN BROWN,** THE AGENT FORMERLY KNOWN AS **DYNAMO,** IS SET FOR A LIFE OF RELAXATION AND CALM--BUT WHO WILL HE SHARE IT WITH?

"LEN FINDS LOVE"

SEE, THIS IS THE LIFE FOR ME... NICE AND QUIET, OUT FOR A PEACEFUL WALK, NOT A CARE IN THE WORLD!

"DON'T GET ME WRONG, I'LL MISS MY OLD PALS THE T.H.U.N.D.E.R. AGENTS--AND SAVING THE WORLD EVERY DAY--BUT I KNOW I DID THE RIGHT THING!"

STILL, THIS LIFE CAN BE LONELY ON YOUR OWN, SO I'VE DECIDED IT'S TIME TO SETTLE DOWN! AND THIS GIRL IS SOMEONE I JUST CAN'T GET OFF MY MIND!

THE HERO DYNAMO IS CERTAINLY NO STRANGER TO ROMANCE, BUT WHICH WOMAN IS HE TALKING ABOUT?
COULD IT BE THE ADVENTUROUS KITTY, FROM THE T.H.U.N.D.E.R. SQUADRON?
OR IS IT THE CHARMING ALICE, FROM LEN BROWN'S DAYS WORKING BEHIND A DESK?

I CAN ONLY HOPE SHE STILL HAS FEELINGS FOR ME, AND AGREES TO MEET LIKE I SUGGESTED!

AND SO OUR GUY GOES ABOUT PLANNING THE PERFECT EVENING FOR HIS MYSTERY GAL!
NOTHING IS TOO GOOD FOR THIS LOVELY LADY, WHOEVER SHE MAY BE!
AND NOW IT'S OFF TO THEIR PLANNED RENDEZVOUS SPOT!
ALL THIS TROUBLE... I SURE HOPE SHE GOT MY MESSAGE!

AND SO LEN BROWN WAITS...BUT FOR WHOM?

WELL HELLO THERE, HANDSOME. IS THIS SEAT TAKEN?
ER, YES, ACTUALLY. I'M WAITING FOR SOMEONE!

OH REALLY? WELL, WAIT NO LONGER!
RUSTY, IS IT REALLY YOU?!

TO OUR SURPRISE, THE WOMAN LEN'S CHOSEN IS NONE OTHER THAN...THE IRON MAIDEN HERSELF!
IN THE FLESH, HANDSOME!

AT LAST! I'VE WAITED SO LONG FOR THIS!
I CAN'T BELIEVE IT'S REALLY HAPPENING! MY DREAM COME TRUE!

BUT LEN, WHAT WILL WE DO? I'M STILL A WANTED WOMAN, TECHNICALLY SPEAKING!
WE'LL GO SOMEWHERE NO ONE WILL EVER FIND US, AND START A NEW LIFE TOGETHER! MAYBE EVEN HAVE SOME CHILDREN! TELL ME, HOW DOES AUSTRALIA SOUND?

OH, LEN, I'VE NEVER BEEN SO HAPPY BEFORE! BUT CAN YOU EVER FORGIVE ME FOR ALL THE HORRIBLE THINGS I'VE DONE? I'M SO AFRAID YOU'LL COME TO YOUR SENSES AND LEAVE ME!

NONSENSE, BEAUTIFUL. YOU AND I WERE MEANT TO BE TOGETHER, AND THAT'S THAT!

AND WITH THAT, OUR HERO AND HIS GIRL ARE OFF. WHO KNOWS WHAT THE FUTURE MAY HOLD, BUT FOR NOW, WE CAN ONLY HOPE THESE TWO LOVEBIRDS FIND THE HAPPINESS THEY DESERVE.
THANKS FOR READING ANOTHER FANTASTIC DOUBLE FEATURE OF T.H.U.N.D.E.R. AGENTS, GANG! IT'S YOUR SUPPORT AND LOYALTY THAT MAKES THESE STORIES WORTH TELLING. JOIN US AGAIN FOR T.H.U.N.D.E.R. AGENTS VOLUME 2!

T.H.U.N.D.E.R. AGENTS #1 variant cover by **Darwyn Cooke**

For the first six issues of T.H.U.N.D.E.R. Agents, each cover image was inspired by a cover from the original 1960s T.H.U.N.D.E.R. Agents series.

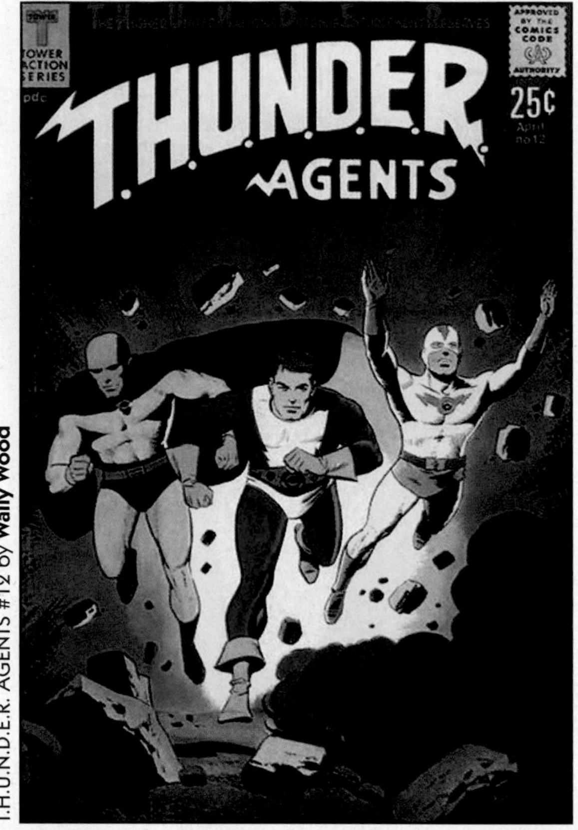

T.H.U.N.D.E.R. AGENTS #12 by **Wally Wood**

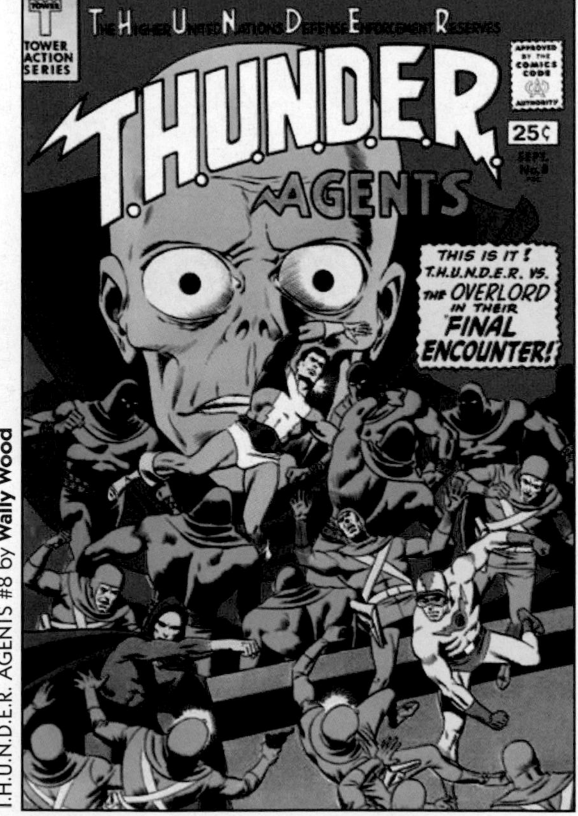

T.H.U.N.D.E.R. AGENTS #8 by **Wally Wood**

T.H.U.N.D.E.R. AGENTS #7 by **Wally Wood** & **Dan Adkins**

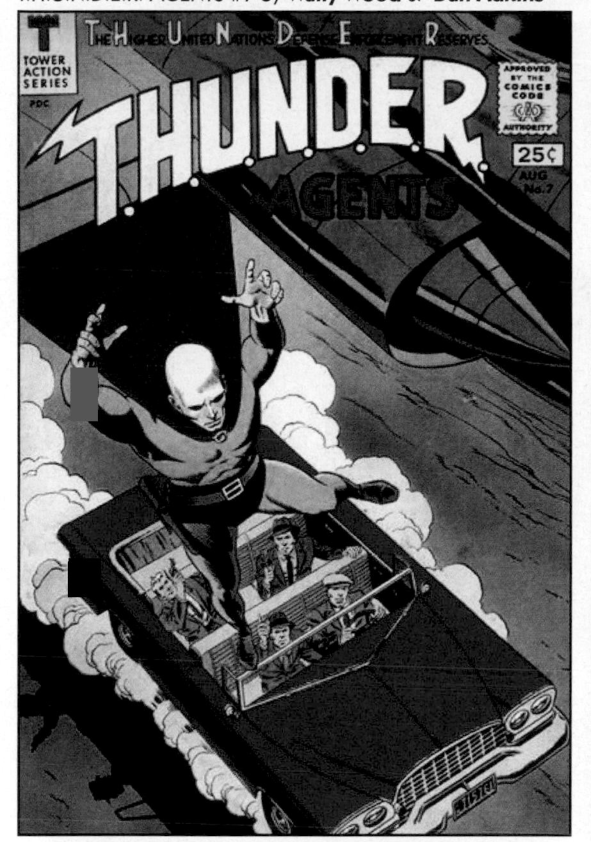

DYNAMO #2 by **Wally Wood** & **Dan Adkins**

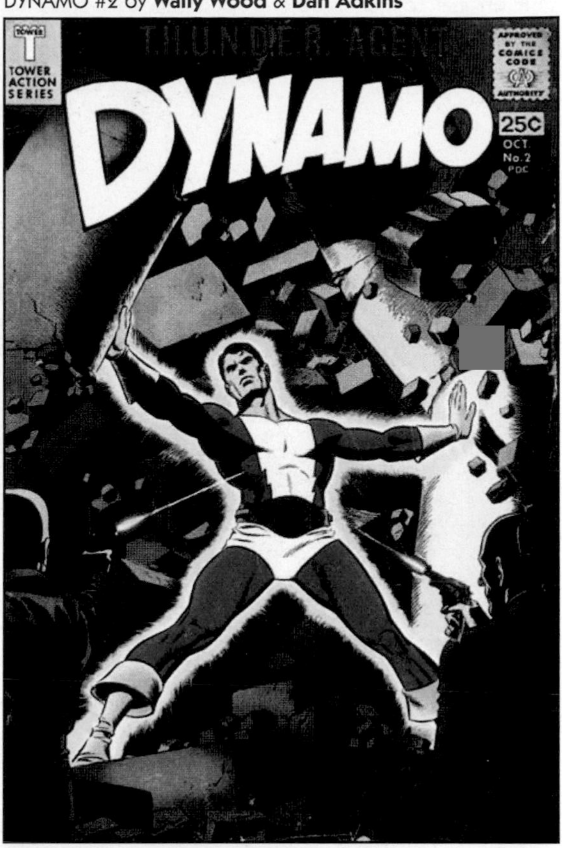

T.H.U.N.D.E.R. Agents MENTHOR collection cover by **Steve Ditko**, **Wally Wood** & **Dan Adkins**

T.H.U.D.E.R. Agents #3 by **Wally Wood**

Series artist CAFU was tasked with coming up with designs that looked very modern yet still paid homage to the original '60s series. Several options for each character were presented (except for NoMan, who kept his original costume), including multiple helmet variations for Menthor and Lightning.

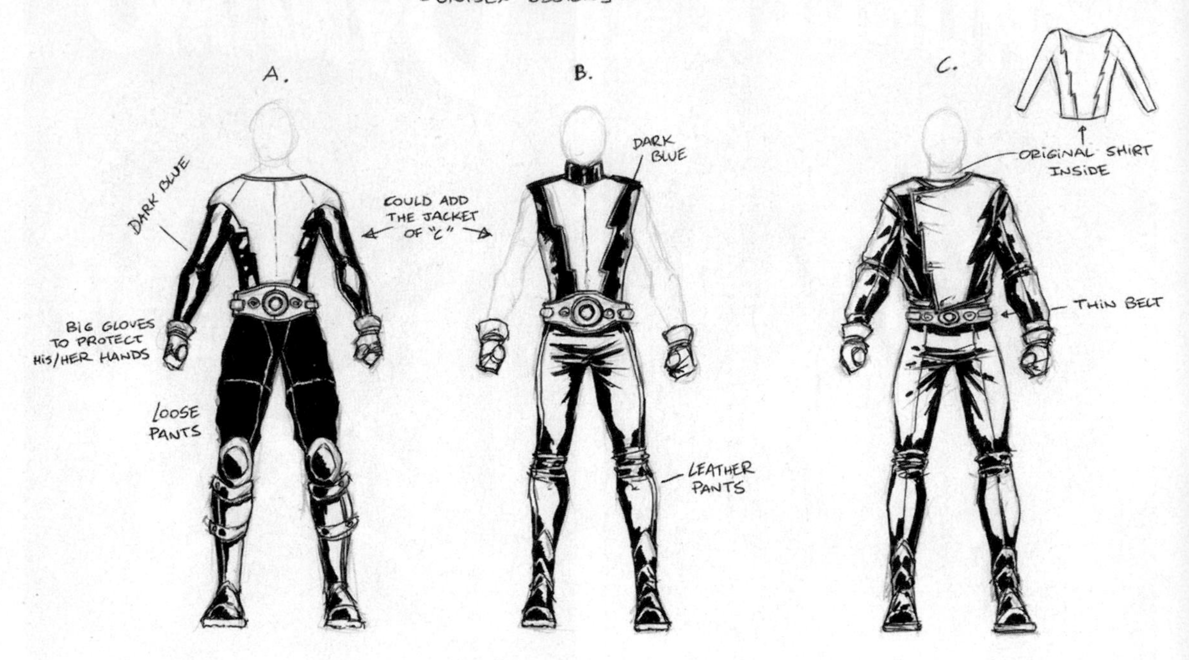

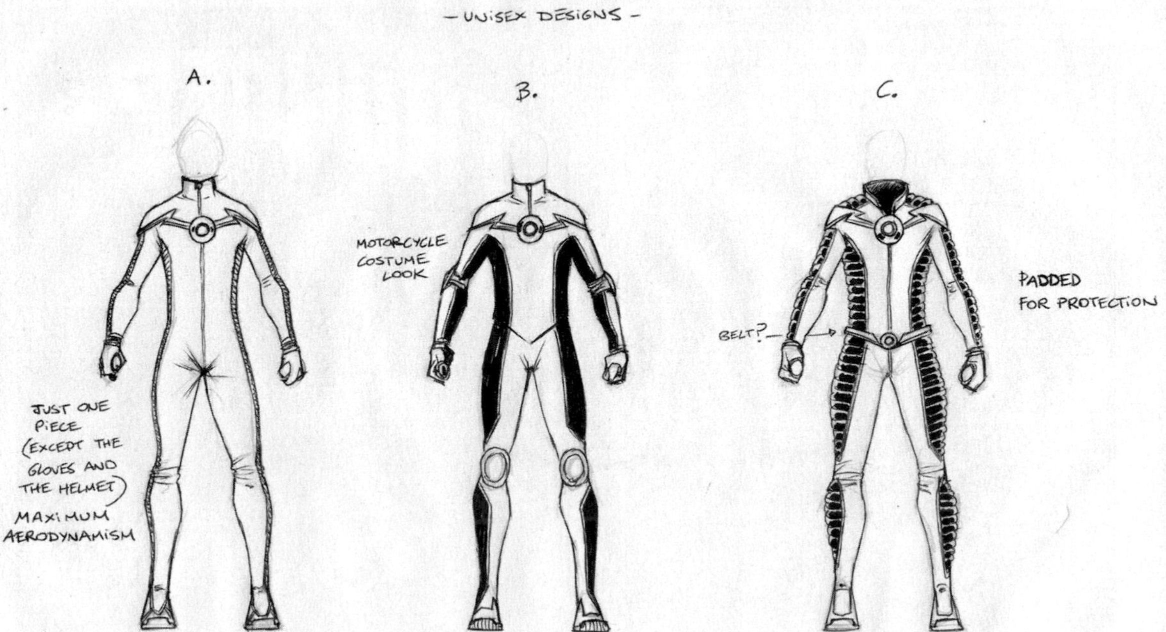

MENTHOR

OPTION A.

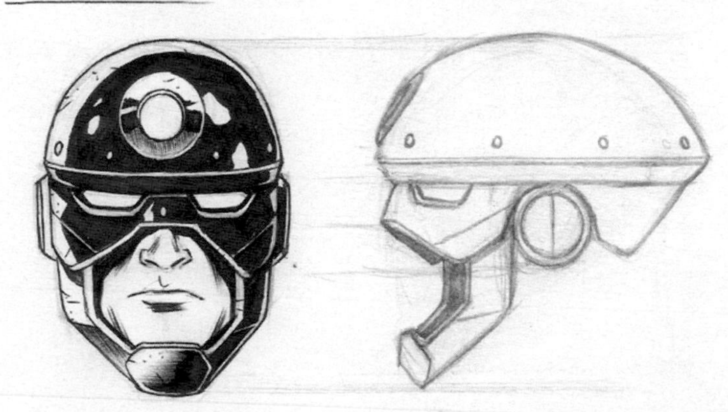

A REAL HELMET
INSTEAD OF
A MASK

(A LITTLE BIT BIG
FOR TOBY'S HEAD)

OPTION B

AVIATOR LOOK

OPTION C

ANTMAN LOOK

OPTION D

PLAIN IRON MASK (RED AND BLUE, LIKE THE ORIGINAL MASK)

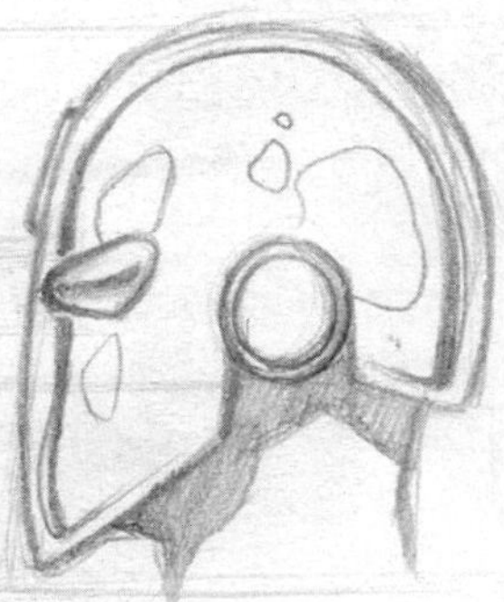

OPTION H

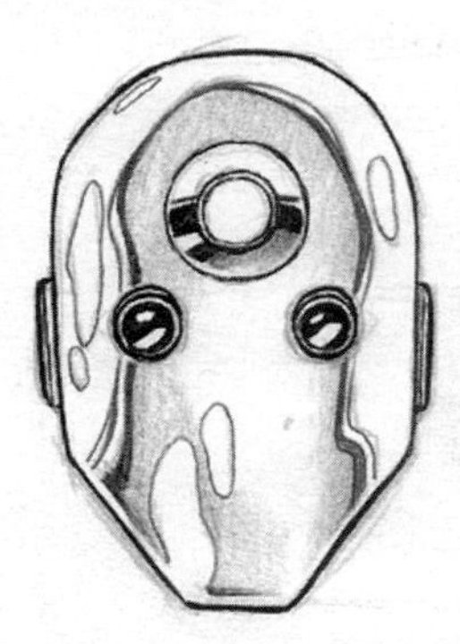

VARIATION ON OPTION D

THIN AND FIBROUS. (MAYBE THINNER AND THINNER AS HE USES HIS POWERS, SHOWING IT SUBTLY)

(OR OLDER)

PADDED

LIGHTNING

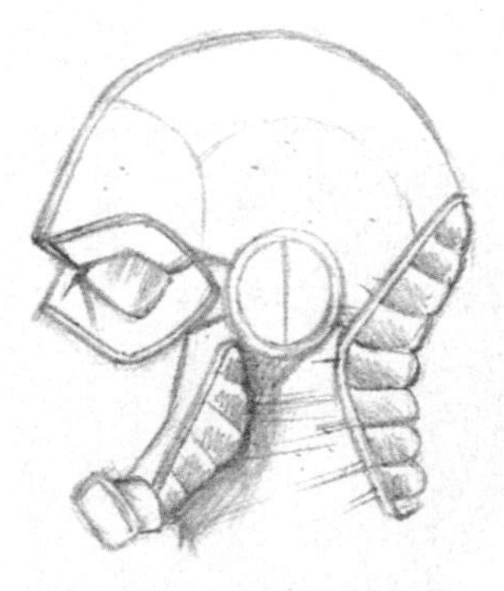

LEATHER MASK WITH AVIATOR GLASSES

OPTION A

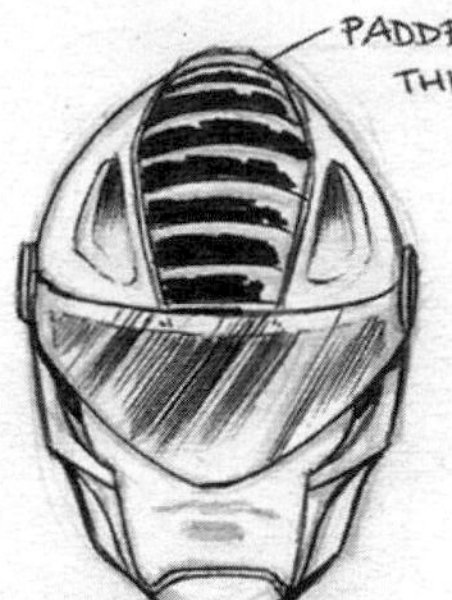

OPTION B

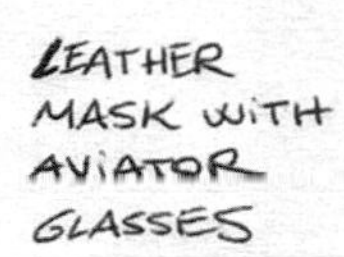

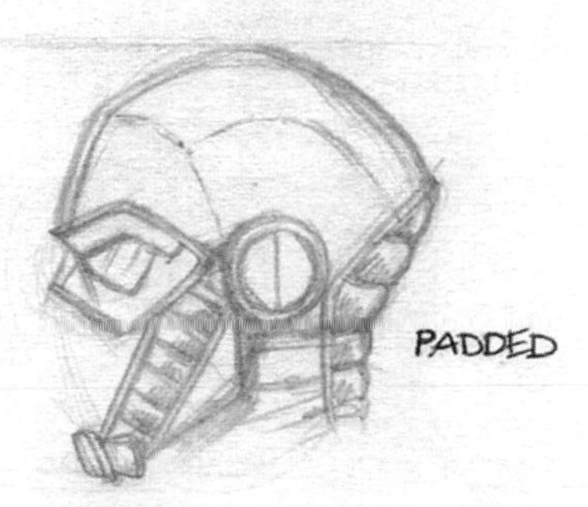

OPTION C

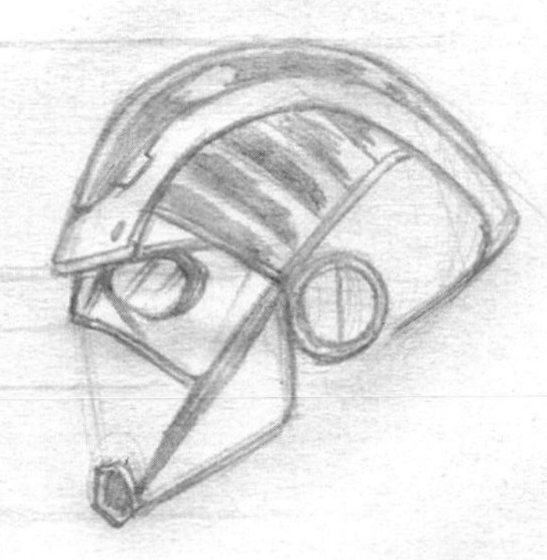

HE LOOKS LIKE
BRUCE WILLIS ON
"UNBREAKABLE"
(EVEN HIS
PHYSIQUE)
ALWAYS
MYSTERIOUS
AND
SHADOWY

HE USES HIS
CAPE AS A
RAINCOAT TO
HIDE HIS
ORIGINAL
COSTUME
(WHICH IS VERY
WORN AND
OLD)

CAPE
BIG HEIGHT

NoMan

HE'S BIG
BUT NOT VERY
MUSCULAR
(AND NOT AS
BIG AS
NOMAN)
HE DOESN'T HAVE
THE PERFECT AND
CLEAN SUPERHERO
LOOK
DARK
BLUE

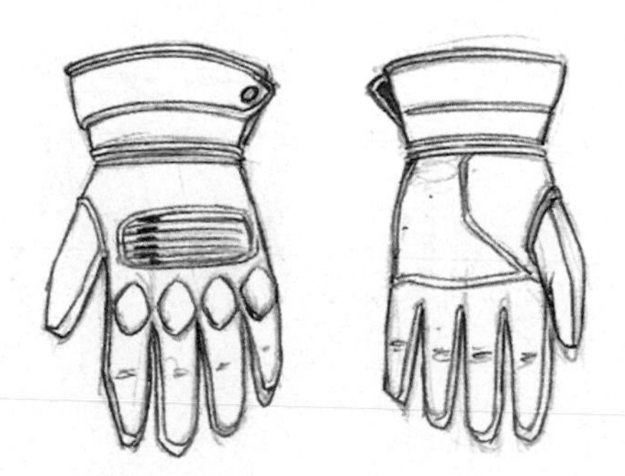

DYNAMO

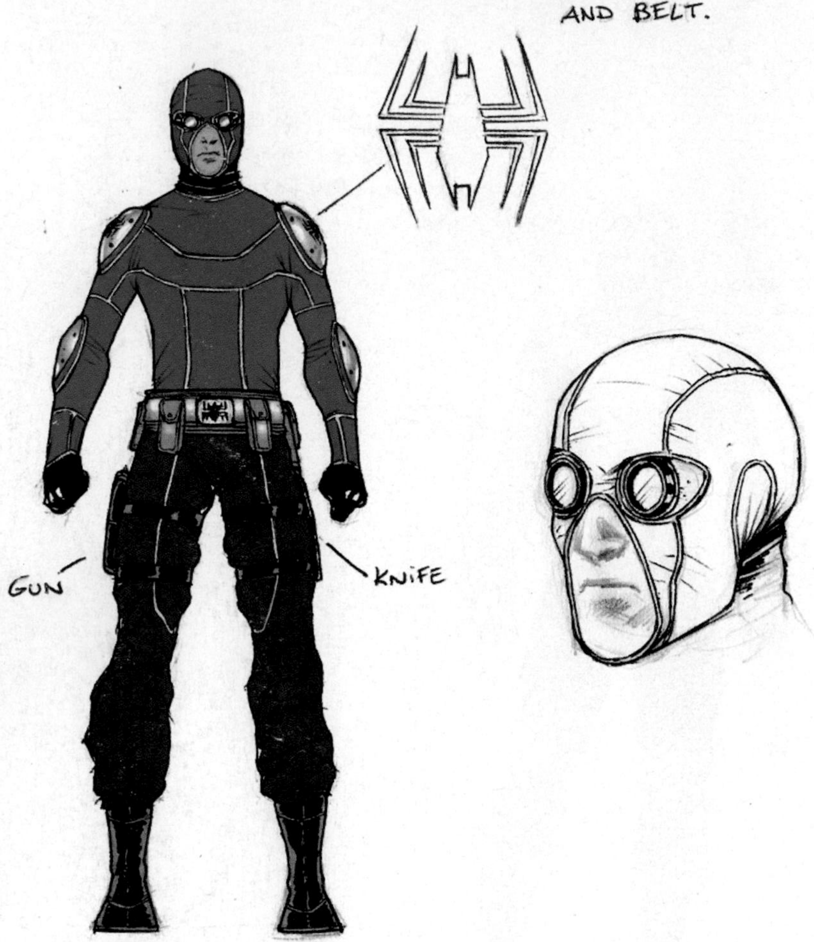
SPIDER SYMBOL
ON SHOULDER PLATES
AND BELT.
GUN
KNIFE

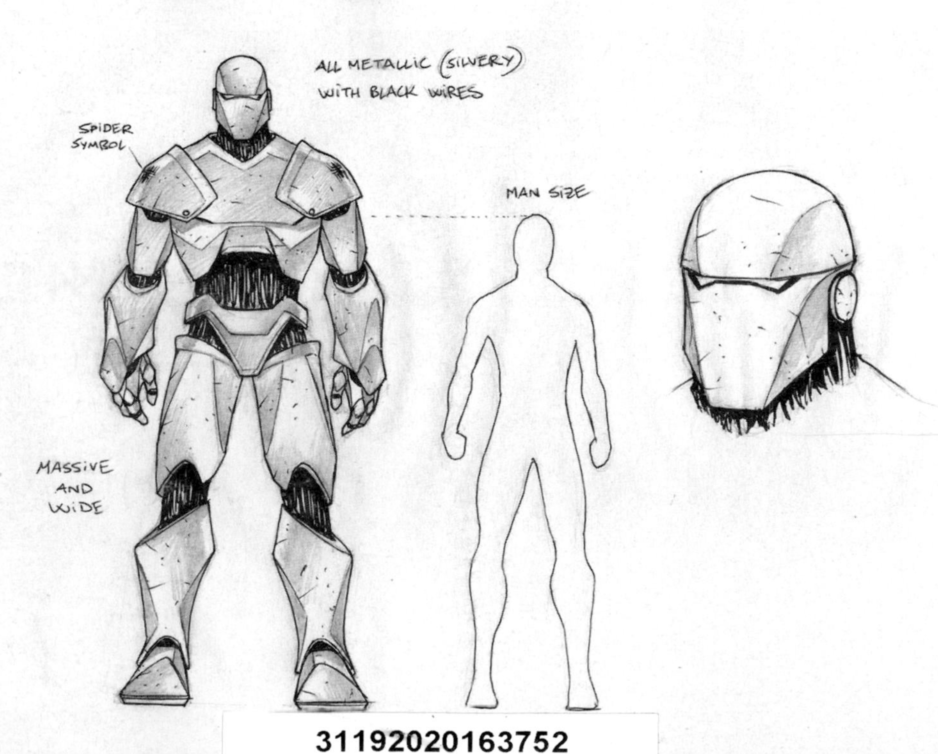
ALL METALLIC (SILVERY)
WITH BLACK WIRES
SPIDER
SYMBOL
MAN SIZE
MASSIVE
AND
WIDE